CW01084672

Legendary Self-Discipline:

Lessons from Mythology and Modern Heroes on Choosing the Right Path Over the Easy Path

By Peter Hollins,
Author and Researcher at
petehollins.com

Table of Contents

Legendary Self-Discipline: *Lessons from Mythology and Modern Heroes on Choosing the Right Path Over the Easy Path* **3**

Table of Contents **5**

The Crucial Ingredient **7**

Section One. Lessons from the Heroes of Old **13**

    Pandora's Box and the practice of discretion and patience in the pursuit of knowledge **15**

    Daedalus and Icarus and the merits of moderation **29**

    Athena and Arachne and the saboteur that is ego **44**

    The Monkey's Paw and the dangers of shortcuts **55**

    Hercules and the Twelve Labors and embracing hardship **69**

Section Two. Masters from the Modern World **84**

    Viktor Frankl and creating self-meaning **86**

    Marc Zupan and overcoming by doing.......... **99**

    Jean-Dominique Bauby and the value of time **111**

    Thomas Edison and the pursuit of failure ...**123**

Sir James Dyson and the decision of perseverance..**136**

Stephen King and the defeat of judgment, rejection, and criticism **150**

Benjamin Franklin and ironclad schedules and goals..**160**

The Crucial Ingredient

Perhaps the most quintessential human trait of all is the longing to go further, to know more, or to create at the very limits of human understanding and ingenuity. Since the dawn of time humankind has wanted to improve itself, to gain mastery over the world we live in and develop our inborn talents to the fullest.

From a romantic perspective, this is why we have molded the planet to suit our needs and desires. We are not a species that is often content with our lot in life, and this has led to some of the greatest advances in history.

However, the path to success and self-actualization has never run smooth.

Victory, it would seem, is reserved mostly for those who actively strive for it. There is plenty of advice out there on how to earn more money, gain valuable skills, be more conscious, harder working, more creative, and so on. But anyone who has tried to apply themselves to any worthwhile pursuit knows that it soon comes down to one crucial ingredient: *Self-discipline. Grit. Willpower. The ability to keep going when the going gets tough.*

All the luck and talent in the world mean nothing if these gifts are not skillfully and consistently applied. Earning more money in itself is a simple proposition, *yet not easy.* It's the same with learning how to type faster, or to get into better physical shape. Most of what we want in life is just that—simple, but not easy.

Luckily, if we are attempting to be the best people we can be, we can turn to those who have gone before us and left behind words of wisdom, caution and encouragement.

Whether these messages come to us in the form of real life uber-successful people or in the stories and fables we tell our children, the lessons are extremely valuable—if we put them into practice. Most of the paths we want to walk down have been blazed already, and there are only a few common threads in each story. For the purposes of this book, we will delve into the will of these people, stories, and myths.

We'll be looking at many such fables, myths and stories from all around the world, as well as the more modern equivalent of real-life people who've found impressive success.

We'll try to extract the key lessons both from those who have "been there and done that," and from the wiser ancients whose insights into the human condition still resonate with us today. Some of these stories and figures you'll be well aware of already, but will be invited to look at with a different perspective, and ask the question, *What one thing do all great people have in common?*

In our book, we'll take a handful of people and figures that don't seem to have much in common on the surface.

And yet, when we unravel their stories, we can make out a few surprisingly common themes. What characteristics mark a person out for success? Not ego, grand ambitions, intolerance for failure and uncertainty or foolish optimism. Rather, it would seem that self-discipline in all its forms is at the core of a well-lived life.

It is self-discipline that encourages us to be patient, to work hard, to be honest with the goals we make for ourselves, to shrug off setbacks and obstacles, to be realistic and mature, and to never expect the good things in life to come to us without hard work.

Some of these figures may naturally inspire you more than others. We all may find differences in the way we engage with the various lessons of vanity, fear, laziness or immaturity. Only *you* can know what skills you're lacking, and only *you* are responsible for their development. Similarly, there is no way to tell what your unique path to self-actualization looks like, but one thing is for sure: you are certain to find the development of self-discipline an invaluable tool along the way.

Section One. Lessons from the Heroes of Old

Though every one of the stories that follow could be interpreted in many ways, we'll be looking at them through a very practical, modern-day lens and asking what they can teach us today about personal development, ethics, discipline, mastery and maturity. These stories are not "true" in the sense that they ever actually took place, but they are true in that they tell us something deep and intimate about the psyches (incidentally, Psyche herself was also a Greek goddess!) of the storytellers.

Can we glean some fundamental truths about human nature by looking at the stories we've been telling ourselves for millennia? Myths are potent, mysterious and have very dark, distant origins in the human mind and in our history. Reading them is a little like shifting through architectural ruins and imagining the places that people built for themselves in the past, and why.

Can we see any echoes of our own humanity in these ancient stories? And if so, can we learn any powerful lessons from our distant ancestors about how to live a wise, fulfilled and moral life?

Pandora's Box and the practice of discretion and patience in the pursuit of knowledge

In Greek mythology, Pandora was the first human female, and she was made from earth and water in the workshop of Hephaestus, the god of metalworking, masonry and sculpture. Zeus had asked her to be made in an effort at revenge after Prometheus had stolen fire from the gods and given it to humanity. The pantheon of gods all gave gifts to the new woman, whose very name means "all gifts."

Aphrodite, the goddess of love, gave her beauty, and Athena, the goddess of wisdom and war, gave her intelligence. Zeus, however, gave her the most curious gift of all: a stone jar (subsequently described as a "box") that he told her to never, ever open.

Zeus then sent Pandora with all her gifts to Epimetheus, Prometheus's brother. Expecting revenge, Prometheus had told his brother never to accept any gifts from Zeus, but as you can guess, he welcomed Pandora and she then failed to resist and opened the jar to see what was in it.

Flooding out of the jar came all the evils of the world: sickness, death, hatred, hunger, fear, sadness... Pandora quickly tried to close the box, but it was already too late. She had "opened a can of worms" and everything had already escaped. By the time she closed it, there was only one thing left inside: hope. Evil and pestilence had been let out into the fresh world, and for what?

How should we interpret this myth today, thousands of years after its first telling? Scholars have picked apart the exact meaning, but we will likely have no need for the academic details here. The fable is certainly an evocative one, bringing to mind themes of Eve eating the forbidden fruit, or of Bluebeard's wife opening a door in the castle she was told never to enter. It may even call to mind the story of Sleeping Beauty, who is also gifted many virtues of supernatural origin, as well as a curse from a more malicious source.

We can wonder at the nature of the gifts—beauty and wisdom naturally seem like wonderful things, but in gifting a jar of evils, was Zeus intending these things to merely bedevil humankind or are they, in a way, gifts as well? This is made more curious still by the fact that hope is included as one of the evils, and it does not make it out into the world—is having hope an essentially good or bad thing?

Though we will miss certain nuances here (our intention is not to conduct an academic analysis of the classics) we can engage with this myth as it stands, seeing what ideas and emotions it evokes in us.

There are perhaps two interpretations here that may spring to mind. The first is that the evils of the world have come to be because of a flaw in a character who does not obey orders and do what they're told. Pandora simply doesn't listen. It's not that she's a bad person, she's simply too curious. The gods, making their wishes clear, forbid Pandora from certain kinds of knowledge (just as Eve is forbidden from eating from the tree of the *knowledge* of good and evil). But who wants to be told that there is something in the world they are not allowed to know—especially when no reason is given for this rule?

Unable to control herself, Pandora's curiosity compels her to trespass and break a rule imposed on her by a higher authority. For this she is punished, and the lesson is clear: do as you're told, rein in your nosiness and you'll remain blissfully unaware of the bad things in life.

In fact many myths and stories take this shape: the protagonist is too inquisitive for their own good, and wants to *know* things that are forbidden to them, only to be punished when they really experience that knowledge. The idea is that there is innocence in ignorance, but that knowledge is somehow painful. You can probably relate to this on some level—we have the tale of a nosy wife who wished she hadn't pried in her husband's secrets, or the shadowy CIA agent who tells us, *You can't handle the truth*.

The other interpretation is a little more subtle. Zeus only embarks on this caper because he is already angry at how much humans know—they've received the fire of the gods which was forbidden to them (and Prometheus has much in common with Pandora in breaking rules to spread knowledge).

Zeus did not merely unleash evils on the world, which he could have easily done. Rather, he gave humankind the *choice*. He must have known that in forbidding them, in concealing the evils in a jar, Pandora would open it willingly and unleash the evils on herself. This could well be seen as a punishment, but we can also see these things as a kind of gift.

The allegory can suggest that something in humankind propels us to learn, to grow and find out more—in other words to be curious! It doesn't matter if we are forbidden, or if higher authorities tell us not to. In fact, this might increase the appeal! *But there is a price for knowledge.* There is always a sacrifice, and nothing comes for free.

Unlike the "good" gifts, which can be received easily as they are, the "bad" gifts come about as a result of free will. In learning more about the world, our eyes open, we cannot unsee what we have seen, and sometimes the things we learn may be very upsetting. Human progress, driven by curiosity, the desire to know and understand more and more, leads to the evils of the world. It's akin to being expelled from Eden after learning "the truth."

This can be seen as a lesson in maturity. Every parent wants to protect their innocent child from learning about the world too fast, from absorbing information that may be too much for them too soon. This myth is a stern warning about respecting the fact that knowledge often comes with a price. It is both a tale of what happens when you don't obey wiser authorities, but perhaps also a lesson in how these things are inevitable—children often have to try out something for themselves to learn, and in learning that lesson, they incur some pain.

If we bluster ahead merely because we have the free will to do so, merely because we cannot contain our curiosity, we may wade into territory that we are not equipped to deal with, and make choices we cannot undo.

What is the correct attitude to learning, to progress and development? Humankind has been making advances—scientific, social and even spiritual—since the beginning of time. But some of these advances can be said to have come at an enormous price. Developments in physics are the result of an insatiable curiosity on the part of the scientists, but were used to create the atom bomb, poisons, new and deadly weapons, machines for control and torture—all things that can be said to be "evils" to humanity.

We cannot go back, just as Pandora cannot put any of the world's evils back in the jar. But many of us would say that even though development and progress is sometimes marred with poor judgment, harsh lessons and horrible realizations that can't be undone—we wouldn't necessarily *want* them to be undone. In other words, the cost was worth it.

In our own lives, we can approach our personal development with a similar degree of consciousness and maturity: rushing ahead before we truly understand something or before we are ready for it is usually disastrous. We must rein ourselves in and exercise self-discipline. Seeking out knowledge simply because we are curious is fine, but learning must be undertaken with an understanding that sometimes the things we discover can be quite frightening, and will result in a loss of innocence.

This lesson may come across as distinctly old-school to the modern reader. It's the equivalent of an old woman sternly warning you to take heed of your elder's advice, or else. But perhaps this is where the modern, particularly Western reader may most benefit. From our cultural context, progress is often seen as an absolute good, and knowledge is to be sought almost for its own sake, with nobody sparing a thought for the outcomes. The idea is that it doesn't matter whether you *should*, but whether you *can*. But there are many Pandora's boxes that have been opened in such a spirit, and now cannot be closed again.

How can we use this wisdom in our own lives? Curiosity is a wonderful thing, and nobody would suggest you lose all wonder and interest in learning new things. Rather, when you embark on a new project of learning, be wise about it. Are you really prepared and ready for what you may learn? When we forbid young children from watching certain movies, for example, it's not because we want to control them—it's because we want to protect them.

When they are old and mature enough, they can truly process what they see without harm. Can you exercise the same wise discretion for yourself? Self-control and self-discipline are paramount here. They can serve as the mental equivalent of treading carefully on a hike, and making sure you don't embark on terrain you are not physically fit enough to endure.

An obvious, practical, real-world example is that of the nosy spouse. They see their partner's private journal that they are compelled to read, despite knowing it's wrong. Curiosity gets the better of them. They soon know far more than they ever did—but the cost is that the "evils" that come from this knowledge are enough to damage the relationships forever. Consider also someone who asks their friend, "Tell me what you think of my screenplay, I want you to be *really honest*" and then is told, to their heartbreak, that the screenplay is garbage.

On a purely practical level, there is the image of a precocious novice who is told by his teacher to focus on certain tools, techniques or texts that are appropriate to his level. In his arrogance, he rushes ahead and wants to know it all at once. He uses a tool that he can't manage and hurts himself, or reads a text that thoroughly confuses or distresses him, or sets his progress *back* because he suddenly realizes how far he has to go and is demoralized.

Curiosity is good, and so is learning. But self-discipline is invaluable in telling us the *pace* we should take in our development. Though we would like to believe otherwise in our modern and democratic times, not all knowledge is for all people at all times. There are remote and isolated tribes in pockets of the world that governments deliberately forbid any contact with. It's because they know that encountering that much knowledge all at once, essentially millennia of progress in a single lifetime, would completely overwhelm and threaten these tribes. Rather they must be left alone to develop at their own pace.

The wisdom, then, is in knowing one's own limitations and having the discipline to be patient, to direct one's curiosity through the appropriate channels. Try to guard against seeking out knowledge merely because you can't contain your nosiness. Rather, plan your path to wisdom as though you were making your own carefully considered curriculum.

Build on your knowledge in stages, take your time and digest what you learn completely before moving on. Lastly, the biggest lesson may come in the realization that knowledge inevitably brings with it a certain loss of innocence, a certain maturity. Approach this gently, thoughtfully and with awareness, and the "evils" of the world can be seen as lessons that give us wisdom.

Daedalus and Icarus and the merits of moderation

Many of the Greek myths have the same flavor we find in the tale of Pandora's box—warning against going too far, being too arrogant, and trespassing into the realms that more rightly belong to the gods. The famous story of Daedalus and his son Icarus is a prime example, and even today this theme survives in modern stories of special people who "flew too close to the sun" and failed.

The story is simple. Daedalus was a master inventor and designer, trained by the mighty goddess Athena herself, and he was commissioned by King Minos to create a vast and complicated labyrinth.

The purpose of the labyrinth was to forever trap the monster minotaur, who was half bull and half human.

The existence of this aberrant creature is a complex tale in itself—powerful Minos was favored by the gods and given a white bull. They told him to sacrifice it, but he disobeyed, and in revenge the gods caused Minos's wife to fall in love with the white bull, producing their monster child, the minotaur. To hide his shame, Minos needed a place to put this creature, and this is where Daedalus and his son come in.

Having completed this glorious maze, however, King Minos imprisoned father and son inside it (Minos is clearly not the most ethical of characters!) to prevent anyone learning about the labyrinth at all. But crafty Daedalus concocted a plan on how to escape. Gathering feathers from birds and sticking them together with wax to make wings, the pair designed their escape—they would fly out of the maze.

As they made their escape, wise Daedalus warned his son not to fly too close to the sun because the warmth would melt the wax and disintegrate his wings. They succeeded for some time, but after they passed Delos Island, Icarus forgot the warning and flew higher and higher. As Daedalus predicted, the sun melted the wax, the wings broke, and poor Icarus fell to the sea and drowned.

This myth is a powerful one because it so clearly and simply explains rather complex ideas of overambition and human egotism. The warning takes the symbolized shape of flying "too high."

In many languages and myths, those who are "down to earth," "salt of the earth" or with their "feet firmly on the ground" are practical, realistic, and straightforward types. It's the idea of *ascension* that belongs to lofty goals, rising up to new, better heights, grand visions and glorious achievements. These things are symbolized in all human psyches as belonging to the inviting but frightening realms of the air. Haven't we all looked at the birds and dreamt that one day we, too, could break the earth's hold on us and soar freely like them?

But in this story, ascension—especially when it is unwise and unchecked—leads to disaster. Not only does Icarus fall back to earth, his fall kills him entirely. In going too high, we are punished and made to fall an equal distance back down again. We see modern-day Icarus characters all around us in the form of celebrities who rise to meteoric fame only to be dashed down to earth through one scandal or another, seemingly punished with a fall that corrects their overambitious ascent. Precocious child prodigies, overnight millionaires or superstar entrepreneurs have all charted this path of *too high too soon*.

In interpreting this story, we can see that it's not flight per se that is dangerous. Finding a clever and innovative way to solve problems is not strictly punishable, since the wise and crafty Daedalus survives using the very same tools and plan that his son does. He succeeds, perhaps, because he uses his wings purely as a tool to escape his predicament. He understands the limitations of these wings, and respects them. A crucial part of the story that is often left out is the extra piece of advice Daedalus gives to his son—that he is not to fly too *low* either, or the water will make his wings heavy and pull him down.

So, what was the nature of Icarus's mistake? Why did he have to pay his life for this mistake? Icarus does not use the wings purely as a tool. He doesn't remain cognizant of their limitations— *his* limitations—and forgets the wise advice of his father. Can you picture young Icarus, whooping and soaring and feeling like a king after being trapped in the dungeon-like maze? Can you imagine the thrill of having wings? It's easy to think of the youth forgetting that the wings are there to help him escape, and instead getting caught up in the delight of flying, showing off, "spreading his wings" and daring himself to greater and greater delights in the air.

In other words, Icarus allowed his ego to overtake his common sense. His ambitions are understandable, but they were unbalanced, overreaching. They took him past his own limitations.

His was a failure to maintain moderation—why? Perhaps, in tasting a little bit of freedom and the thrill of flying, he was seduced to greater and greater heights, well out of the bounds of the normal and practical. This elevated range is not sustainable. The heat of the sun (an eternal symbol of something godlike, rarified, ultimately powerful, life giving but not safe to stare directly at!) is too strong and destroys his wings.

The wings here are the very things that allow him to reach the heights in the first place, but are undermined by too sharp an ascent. A modern parallel is a young rock star whose brilliant talent allows him a steep rise to fame. But he keeps on rising, getting closer and closer to his own "sun," until the rigors of fame (exhaustion, drug use, poor mental health, money squabbles, family trouble, etc.) start to corrode the very talent that allowed him to find success in the first place. He "falls."

A person suffering bipolar disorder may experience this same arc regularly—seduced by the sun in the form of overambitious and lofty goals, only to find the heights are unsustainable—and it's a long, long way down.

Icarus's behavior is a warning to us all. We can imagine Daedalus trying to teach his son—yes, it's tempting to go as high as you can, to stretch your abilities to the limit and beyond, but you need to respect your limitations or be destroyed by them. It may seem far more fun to go all-out, have grand plans and epic dreams, but in the long run these ambitions may actually be less sustainable than a path forged more moderately.

The question of moderation turns up frequently, and not just in Greek mythology. The wise path is frequently the *middle* one: like Goldilocks' perfect porridge, it's not too hot or too cold. It's just right. An implied corollary lesson in the tale of Icarus is that it would be just as bad to fly too low. Those people who have too few ambitions and who plod along too close to the earth can also suffer because of it. You get bogged down and perish all the same if you never challenge yourself, never rise to the occasion, never follow your dreams but instead stick close to the path well-trod by others.

The best way is seldom the biggest, best, flashiest and most dramatic one. The best technique is rarely to go all out. Rather, it's a question of appropriateness. Of balance and a light touch to discern when to push and when to hang back. The truly successful in life, the tale seems to suggest, know how to practice self-control and restraint, tempering the human urge to vault into the unknown without a care in the world.

How can we apply these principles to our own lives, especially when it comes to moderation? It can be tricky when we live in a world that in many ways encourages epic and unsustainable levels of success. Surrounding us are stories and images of impossibly beautiful women, impossibly wealthy men, impossibly skillful scientists and creators, impossibly talented athletes and impossibly intelligent philosophers... We tell our children to dream big and lap up stories of rags to riches and the American Dream, telling us that an ordinary person can and even should aspire to the absolute peak of achievement.

Not only does the intensity of this ambition frequently backfire (how many of us actually achieve it?) but for the few that "succeed," the intensity is often damaging. We don't hear as often the stories of successful entrepreneurs who have sacrificed *everything* at the altar of business, including relationships, physical health, even their sanity. We forget about the stars after they burn out and retreat. Ours is a culture that encourages people to always be more, more, more.

The irony is that the more measured, mature (and to some, more boring!) approach actually has the better chance of lasting success and happiness. Fly, but not too close to the sun. Strive, develop and have goals—but temper these with realistic restraint. Daedalus never forgets what he is meant to be doing: escaping to safety. It's this that is at the front of his mind, and not the wings themselves. Icarus's downfall could also be a warning against narcissism and vanity.

By becoming enamored with his own ability to fly, Icarus forgets what the wings are actually there for. Thus, an author that finds sudden and spectacular fame may get a big head and start to view his art more as ego stroking for his vanity, and not about the writing itself.

To combat this sort of waywardness, we have to consistently be aware of and resist the temptation to go further than we should—or can. In all your goals and dreams, can you be honest with yourself and ask what proportion of the goal is simply for your own self-glorification? Have you ever tasted a little success and then ran with it, well beyond your limits? Self-discipline is difficult, and it's most difficult to conjure up in the moments it's most needed: those times when we feel seduced by the "big lights" of our own grand narcissism, the temptation to be a star in our own lives, to have a grand, thrilling life. This is, essentially, an immature state of mind, and one that the older Daedalus knows to ward against.

A young man could be raised up out of poverty by being selected for a sports scholarship. He is praised by others and soon starts to enjoy the attention, relishing in his own natural talents and pushing himself further. He achieves some success and almost becomes addicted to it. Why not expand? He could put his name to popular brands to make more money. He finds himself "living large" and going into debt to live in princely homes, indulging in expensive and unsustainable habits.

He stars in cameo roles on TV, his ego growing day by day. Some warn that he has forgotten his roots, and has lost touch with reality. He starts dabbling with politics, fancying himself as a businessman and philanthropist who wants to use his money to invest and start foundations and scholarships...

You already know the end to the story! However, you don't have to actually live a dazzling tale like this to derive value from the Icarus story. Every time you ignore your own limits in order to strive for some lofty goal purely for your own ego, you are like Icarus, failing to heed the advice of moderation. A good technique is to constantly maintain awareness of your motivations, and your real goals. Icarus could have done well to remember what he was doing—escaping. Don't forget your own goals. What are you truly after? Don't get distracted from that, no matter what tempting offers come to sidetrack you.

Truly masterful and accomplished people know that the ego and naïve, youthful ambition can actually get in the way of achievement, rather than support it. Take yourself out of the equation and never forget to ask how you can be better, no matter how much success you feel you have and want to celebrate. Be moderate and measured.

Drop notions of godlike glory and fame—you may feel like a champion for pulling an all-nighter working on your brilliant new business idea, but you'd be better off living a more balanced lifestyle, channeling your excitement appropriately. The choice may be between one all-nighter followed by a crash and a completely failed project, or a week of patient, balanced workdays and a successful project.

"Pride comes before a fall" goes the old wisdom. Being too attached to the outcome of a goal can ironically undermine your performance. If you think of truly brilliant and accomplished people in this world (not the momentary celebrities, but the lifelong masters), their approach is slow-and-steady, and they work on their goal for the goal's sake, not for their own glorification. They aren't superstars, and they're not failures, but rather they have found that perfectly moderate Goldilocks zone in the middle.

Athena and Arachne and the saboteur that is ego

Let's take a closer look at ego and how it can undermine even genuine talent. You don't have to be a student of the Greek classics to notice that many of the myths have a consistent theme in the supposed correct relationship of humans to the gods: obedient, humble and deferential. There are many stories of what happens when mere mortals fail to know their place, but one of the most striking is the story of Athena and Arachne.

Arachne was a shepherd's daughter, who from a young age showed astounding skill at weaving. However, she was a boastful woman and didn't acknowledge that her talents stemmed from, in part, the goddess Athena, who was patroness of weaving. To teach Arachne a lesson, Athena challenged her to a contest, but allowed her to gracefully bow out to save face. Arachne refused to step down, claiming that she was the best weaver and could beat even the goddess herself. Her attitude was what the ancient Greeks called hubris—an overreaching sense of arrogance.

At the contest, Athena weaved classical scenes of the god's rebuking and punishing mortals who believed themselves on their level. Arachne depicted the god Zeus deceiving, tricking and even seducing mortals—a very cheeky statement indeed. The goddess, seeing this and noting also that Arachne's work was indeed better than hers, was furious. She destroyed the weaving and struck Arachne, who was so ashamed that she soon hanged herself. Athena's stern punishment was to turn Arachne into a spider (indeed her name means spider in ancient Greek), so she could spin for all eternity.

What are we to make of this tale? Here it's important to note that the historical and cultural nuances of this story are complex, and carry themes of provoking authority and perhaps even a satirical poke at what was autocratic rule by Emperor Augustus at the time. Nevertheless, we can adapt this tale for more modern tastes quite easily.

Though few today will claim to seriously believe in "the gods," the truth is that we do function with a fixed idea of external authorities that rule over our lives—our "gods" could be government, the various powers that be, "the rich," the culture at large and its norms and values, the economy, the law, even natural scientific principles that are felt to reign over us in a more or less non-negotiable way.

By seeing the allegorical gods in Greek myths more as ideas, archetypes and beliefs, we can begin to uncover more depth to the story. Arachne's transgression is clear: she's arrogant, and immature. Her overconfidence allows her to see herself as the sole cause of her success, rather than acknowledging that luck, fate or the support of others might have played a role, too.

Rather than being grateful for her abilities, she is cocky and boastful. She is like a student who precociously challenges their master, completely forgetting that the master has taught them so much of what they know, or a cheeky young child mocking his parents for being boring and uncool, not realizing that his parents are that way in part because they've worked so hard to provide for him!

A crucial detail in this story is that *Arachne is actually right*—she is a better weaver than the goddess and proves it. She accurately shows an unflattering portrait of Zeus himself, criticizing his behavior to mortals. But this does nothing to stop the outcome of the story. In fact the goddess, doubly enraged by the impetuosity, punishes her even more harshly where she was willing to forgive in the beginning. Does this really mean that the tale is telling us to fold and submit to higher authorities, even when they are wrong and we are right?

One of the lessons here is an uncomfortable one: being right doesn't necessarily mean you'll get what you want in life. We can imagine a modern-day analogy: a plucky young intern joins a powerful company and starts to challenge the bosses, stepping out of line, disobeying orders and publicly disparaging the entire way the company does business.

He may well be right, but those in charge aren't likely to respond well to his attitude, and he may quickly find himself out of a job and even blacklisted. The fact that he legitimately knew better won't figure into the story—it's his nerve and condescending attitude that earn him a smiting from the "gods." The intern fails to properly understand that his role in the organization, his salary and his position, all come from those higher up.

He may not agree with everything they say, but it is certainly unwise to flagrantly challenge them. Ultimately they still have the power, just as Athena has the power to completely destroy Arachne, whether she won the contest or not.

This interpretation can seem a little discouraging to those who like to imagine that the world always rewards truth and honesty, but again here the more subtle message is the power of patience, moderation and self-control. Arachne simply doesn't think about what she's doing. She knows she's right, she's prideful and full of herself, and never stops to imagine how things may play out for her.

Let's imagine the gods and goddesses as more abstract principles. Have you ever known anyone who railed and fought relentlessly against, for example, the government, religion, culture, the law, other people in general? Those people who always felt themselves to be in the right, those know-it-alls who seldom respect others, in particular if those others are in positions of authority? This is a rebellious, haughty person who likes to push back against business as usual, the higher-ups… or anything, really.

If we understand the gods to be symbolic principles of a natural universal order, a person who challenges this is someone who doesn't respect forces greater than himself. Perhaps he's a daredevil with no care for his own mortality, and essentially challenges the gods to a contest every time he performs some reckless stunt.

Maybe he's a haughty scientist who boldly claims that there simply are no "gods," only the rational world of science, which he will soon get the better of using nothing more than his own intellect (a version of the myth that's perhaps a little more relevant for modern audiences?) He might be a person who can't be bothered learning about history or the lessons of his ancestors, and so condemns himself to repeat their mistakes (i.e. he is punished).

In any case, a person who doesn't properly respect the larger order around them, including the rank and position of their "betters," is inviting a serious reprimand. Of course, nobody would suggest that there's no room for challenging the old ways, for innovation, creativity and new ideas. And the myths don't seem to say that the gods are unreasonable or have an illegitimate rule over mortals. Rather, it's a question of *attitude*: Arachne has little self-control and zero humility. Her ego rages over her self-discipline. She is talented, but what does it amount to if she insists on being so haughty about the fact?

We can learn from Arachne and her mistakes. The unfortunate fact is that all of us have to live in a world of hierarchies, and there will always be people in power who we are required to defer to. Beyond that, there are universal laws that we simply cannot push back against, and shouldn't. The myth is not about whether this is wrong or right, however (or indeed about what's "fair"). Rather, it's about the smart way to deal with things. History is littered with people who had genius ideas but who lacked the tact and strategy to get them implemented. Diplomacy and the right attitude can go a very long way!

If the myth of Arachne resonates with you, you might like to get in the self-discipline habit of setting aside the question of who is "right." It's always a good idea in any social interaction to be respectful where it matters, courteous and humble, and understand that even if you *are* right, it's seldom helpful to brag about it.

The mark of maturity is knowing when and how to practice a little self-restraint—and how to hold your tongue even if you're itching inside to prove that you know better! With wisdom, we find the discipline to act in the interests of harmony and good diplomacy, and we trump vanity or our ego's need to feel vindicated. Do you ever carry on and on with an argument, unable to let it go unless you've thoroughly "won" and the other person acknowledges it? Take a page from Arachne's book and let it go.

At the end of the myth, Arachne is no longer human, and is condemned arguably to weave creations that are nowhere near as beautiful as the ones she once made. This is the old advice to never "bite the hand that feeds you."

Arachne, for all her impressive skill, derives her talent from the gods, who can swiftly take it away again.

Arachne's falls from her arrogant position, and her ultimate humiliation is to be stripped of the skills she was so ready to boast about. In the same way, people who are arrogant and barge ahead without a second thought often find themselves in a much-weakened position. A daredevil young person may be overconfident and reckless with their own lives, but in doing so, the gods can take that life away again, showing that it always belonged to them in the first place.

The Monkey's Paw and the dangers of shortcuts

This classic piece of literature is certainly not as old as the Greek myths we've already considered, but it nevertheless contains a theme of warning that wouldn't have been alien to the ancient Greeks. This short story, written by W. W. Jacobs in 1902, has widely been interpreted as a warning against using supernatural means to interfere with the wise hands of fate. There are actually several stories in more modern folklore that tackle the same themes, and the moral of them all seems to be encapsulated in the old adage, "Be careful what you wish for."

The story, very briefly, goes like this.

Mr. White and his son Herbert are playing chess one night when Sergeant-Major Morris comes to visit them. He stays for dinner and afterwards shows them a fascinating artifact he found while serving in the British army in India: a mummified monkey's paw. Morris explains that an Indian fakir had placed a magical spell on the paw so that it would grant the owner three wishes.

He also explains that the paw has brought him nothing but grief, and with that throws it into the fire. Morris warns Mr. White that using the three wishes only brings dire consequences, but Mr. White, intrigued and not heeding the warning, quickly retrieves the paw. Mr. White later decides to wish for the remaining amount left on his mortgage (the equivalent of around $30,000).

The next morning, Herbert the son goes to work and is tragically killed in a machinery accident. The company denies responsibility but makes a payment to the family—a payment of roughly $30,000. The wish has come true, but in the most hideous form. Mrs. White, overcome with grief, demands that Mr. White use another wish to bring their son back (can you see where this is going?). He does so, and an hour later there is a knock at the door, and Mr. White immediately understands that the monster at the door is not really his son at all. He quickly makes the third wish, the knocking outside stops, Mrs. White opens it to find nobody there, and screams out in anguish.

Despite its horror elements, the story has a classic mythical structure to it, with three wishes and an ill-considered tampering with fate, leading to a sort of punishment from the gods themselves. "The Monkey's Paw" will appeal to a modern audience because the lessons in it seem so relatable: who hasn't "wished" for something only to discover that it's not at all what they really wanted?

Let's dig deeper to unravel the useful life lessons within this story. It is, like our previous two tales, a story of transgression and punishment. But what is the nature of Mr. White's crime? He is shown the monkey's paw and told repeatedly that it is dangerous and will result in dire consequences, but ignores these warnings entirely.

Why? It's easy to imagine a few reasons: he is greedy and gets carried away with the endless possibilities, or he is desperate and sees in the paw a way out of his life troubles. Perhaps his failure to take Morris's warnings seriously shows a simple foolishness on his part—why heed any caution when the prospect of getting everything you want is so close at hand?

Whatever it is, Mr. White ignores the warnings and at his own peril. His first wish is for something some might think trivial, given the seemingly unlimited magical power of the paw. He wishes for money, but doesn't say *how* this money will come into being. The horrifying consequence (his son dying in effect to produce this money) seems to be a kind of cosmic lesson in cause and effect— there is "no such thing as a free lunch" and if money were to really magically appear, it would need to come from somewhere.

The menace we see from the monkey's paw seems to be a stern lesson: life is as it is for a reason, and if you interfere without understanding what you're doing, you only bring calamity on yourself.

The theme repeats until the wishes are finished. Arguably Mrs. White's wish is less selfish than her husband's, but she makes the fatal mistake of not learning from his mistake. Rather than destroying the paw there and then, they dig themselves further into the hole by making more wishes—and in the end the only way to get out of the trouble is use the wishes completely and be worse off than they started.

The characters in this story are not bad people, but they lack foresight or a greater vision. It's as though, ignorant of the complex webs of life behind their current situation, they wish for something that is unrealistic, undeserved, almost *unnatural*. Most of us have likely had thoughts of this kind: we wish we could win the lottery, or magically wake up one morning with the body of our dreams and ten years younger, or get a lucky break and become famous overnight. But all these wishes are the antithesis of carefully considered, mature goals that are worked out in the real world while obeying natural laws.

The warning against messing with fate is a profound one—it tells us that we don't always understand why things are as they are, and so cannot always get what we want. In our limited human perspective, it's unwise to pout and wish for reality to be something else, especially when we have no real understanding of the mechanisms underlying this reality. We are not meant to "play god" and toy with the universe of which we are only a part.

A popular Buddhist fable has the same lesson: a farmer one day loses his only horse, and his neighbor says, "How unfortunate for you!" but the farmer only replies, "Maybe, maybe not. We'll see." Later, the horse comes back, and following it is another, better horse. The neighbor now says, "How fortunate for you!" and again the farmer replies, "Maybe, maybe not. We'll see." Later, the farmer's son is injured trying to train this new horse, and the neighbor again chips in, saying how unlucky the farmer is.

The farmer only says, again, "Maybe, maybe not. We'll see." Some time later war is declared and every young man drafted to serve. However the farmer's son, being injured, is exempt and can stay home, surely saving his life. Again the neighbor congratulates the farmer and says how lucky he is, and the farmer, in his wisdom, only smiles and says, "Maybe, maybe not. We'll see..."

The moral of this story is obvious: in our limited perspective, we are never truly in the position to say whether events or circumstances are fortunate or unfortunate, good or bad. Some calamities later turn out to be blessings in disguise, and some gifts are later understood as curses. Many people say that their most painful life challenges taught them the most about life, and many people discover, with a little time and wisdom, that what they *thought* they wanted brought them no happiness at all.

It's this strictly human limitation on perspective that makes us so ill-equipped to decide "fate" is wrong and that we know better. Just as a child who is given the power to decide what to have for dinner might foolishly decide on four bowls of ice cream and be sick, we can't always know the best course for life to take, in the grand scheme of things.

How do we take the lessons from the monkey's paw and put them into practice in real life, though? None of us, thankfully, will have access to a magical yet cursed item that gives us whatever our heart desires. At the end of such stories, the characters have learnt their lesson: there is a heavy load of regret, and the feeling now that they *should have left things just as they were.*

In our own lives, it's important to be realistic and as mature as possible when it comes to deciding our grand dreams and wishes for ourselves. Again, this takes a degree of restraint and self-discipline. On a wild whim we might decide that what we *really* want is to go and live off-grid in the forest somewhere, only to go and find ourselves dangerously unprepared and with all our illusions of that way of life completely shattered. On the other hand, many of us will look at a challenge or failure in our lives and rail against it, calling it a mistake or a punishment that we don't deserve.

But is it really?

The monkey's paw tale reminds us that human beings have limitations, and that it's always better to stick to your realm of control rather than overreach into the supernatural—or in more practical terms, the overly ambitious, unethical or unrealistic. What is our appropriate realm of control? Well, we can always make goals and plans to the best of our knowledge, work hard and honestly to achieve those, and adapt as we go along and learn more. We can have the wisdom and maturity to look at the events in our life and withhold judgment, like the Buddhist farmer; maybe it's a blessing, maybe not. Who's to say? Like Mr. and Mrs. White, when they play God without knowing what they're doing, the results are monstrous.

On a basic level, it's always prudent to hold off on interfering with things you don't understand—especially those that come with explicit warnings. An obvious example is a student who takes an illicit drug to help him cram before an exam, without any care of the inevitable side effects coming his way. Rather than approaching the problem in the "normal" way—studying and doing his best—he tries to cheat and uses a tool he doesn't understand or respect, and suffers the consequences.

We can see echoes of this moral in stories of people being bitterly disappointed to find that the proverbial grass is not in fact greener on the other side, and that there is no way to magically find a shortcut through life.

The classic stories of making a "deal" with the devil are a similar warning—we are lured by the promise of money or fame or luxury, and in our blindness and ignorance we barge ahead, not reading the "fine print"—i.e. that we have sold our souls to get what we wanted. In myths and stories, the person cutting a supernatural deal is always burnt in the end, sometimes on a "technicality" like in the monkey's paw, or sometimes because what the person thought they wanted is soon discovered to be awful (like King Midas, who quickly realizes what a stupid idea it is to turn everything you touch to gold!).

In our own lives, we can become adept at using self-discipline and restraint when we develop goals and dreams. Can we routinely ask what it is we think we want, and be honest about why? Are we acting because we hope to find some kind of cheat code to the game of life? Are we letting ourselves be deceived by something that promises us our wildest dreams without stopping to understand exactly what that means? This could apply to pyramid schemes and poor investments, or to being suspicious of romantic or business partners who promise the world, or to gurus or coaches who claim you can have whatever you want with no effort.

Self-discipline is having the presence of mind to think carefully before your own greed or desire runs away with you. Just like in the Daedalus and Icarus story, the best path is seldom the flashiest one, but more often goes along with ordinary, consistent hard work and an unfailing eye on the goal, despite temptations or flashy promises that end up being worse for you in the long run. It's a lesson in good sense.

"The Monkey's Paw" is on some level just a fun spooky tale, but on another level it's a very deep warning to let go of a foolish desire to boss the universe around. Instead, it's better to cultivate a mature acceptance of life and its hardships, especially those we don't like or understand. Suffering is inevitable, and trying to avoid it never works, or even leads to more suffering. Actions undertaken without any proper understanding of what you're doing can't be expected to work, and at worst can be dangerous.

Rather than foolishly wishing for things to be different, take a wiser, broader view, and resist the urge to decide prematurely what's best. On the most practical level, a wonderful lesson is simply to be patient: sometimes, things resolve themselves merely by you waiting without acting. What was a problem reveals itself in time to be an integral part of a bigger process. Wisdom and self-discipline teach us that interfering in these bigger processes can only lead to trouble.

Hercules and the Twelve Labors and embracing hardship

Even those unfamiliar with Greek mythology will recognize the name Hercules and the twelve near-impossible feats of strength and bravery he was assigned to complete. But few know *why* Hercules labored on these tasks, and what the deeper lesson of the story is.

Context matters here. Hercules was born of Zeus (as so many were—he was a busy deity); however, he was only a *demi*-god, since his mother was Alcmene, a mortal. Zeus was married to the goddess Hera at the time, who was so enraged that she vowed to destroy Hercules, the incarnation of her husband's infidelity. To take revenge she sent snakes to the baby Hercules' crib but the boy, showing incredible strength, simply killed the snakes. He grew to be a strong, successful man who later married and had three strong sons.

Jealous and angry at his success, Hera upped the ante and caused the adult Hercules to fall into an insanity that caused him to kill his own children and wife, Megara. Once the insanity lifted, Hercules was overcome with grief. He sought the counsel of wise Apollo who told him that to redeem himself, he must serve Eurystheus, the king of Tiryns.

Unfortunately, Hera found a way to sneakily suggest that the king assign impossible tasks that would surely kill Hercules. He had to slay a nine-headed Hydra monster. He had to kill the fierce Nemean lion, capture the Erymanthian boar and the Cretan bull, obtain the belt of Hippolyta and several other dangerous or near-impossible feats.

For posterity, the rest of the twelve labors of Hercules were as follows:

- capture the stag of Arcadia
- clean the cattle stables of King Augeas of Elis
- shoot the carnivorous birds of the Stymphalian marshes
- capture the mad bull of the island of Crete
- capture the man-eating mares of King Diomedes of the Bistones
- take the girdle of Hippolyta, queen of the Amazons
- steal the cattle of the three-bodied giant Geryon of the island of Erytheia
- retrieve the golden apples at the world's end guarded by Hesperides
- fetch from the underworld the three-headed dog Cerberus, guardian of the gates of the underworld

No small feats. Astonishingly, Hercules achieved all the tasks, one by one, with his strength, determination and cunning (and a little help from others along the way). Hercules continued to have many escapades after completing his missions, and the ferocious Hera never quite stopped trying to trick, destroy or humiliate him. But eventually, the gods were so impressed with Hercules' strength that they elevated him to a full god.

What can we learn from poor Hercules' seemingly never-ending life troubles and dramas? Like other mythical figures (consider the biblical Job, who similarly has misfortune after misfortune thrown his way), he seems to embody the occasional human suspicion that there's a vengeful god out there constantly trying to mess with us! Sometimes, it feels like life is just one difficulty after another. The myth of Hercules teaches us that we are all, in a way, demi-gods—we have a weaker, fearful and mortal human side but also a stronger, wiser, godlike aspect that can help us triumph over any adversity, if we can follow it rather than give in to the temptation to give up.

In fact, Hercules does face this very decision in a lesser-known story from his childhood. The story of Kakia and Arete tell us a lot about what the myth of Hercules is really all about. It goes like this: In Hercules' youth he was confronted by two very different goddesses.

The first was beautiful, alluring Kakia, who offered Hercules a life of easy pleasure. Though she told him she was called "happiness," her name actually means "vice." Kakia promised a path that was free of pain and hard work, and was filled instead with pleasure and delight, i.e. "the easy way."

You can guess how Arete compared: she was a humble, quiet goddess who told Hercules that *her* path was the only way to genuine happiness and achievement, but it would be long and difficult, even painful at times. Her message was simple: nothing worthwhile in the world was to be gained without hard work and effort.

Pleasure and wisdom had a price, which the wise man understood and paid willingly. Her promise was only that if Hercules wanted to achieve great things, he must learn to master those skills, and he must work for what he wanted—and in laboring for them, they would be worth so much more. Her name meant "virtue" and suggested a life path that was slower, more steadfast, but ultimately the best hope at a good, moral existence—i.e., real happiness. Arete's path was "the hard way."

By his conduct throughout his life, we already know which path Hercules ultimately chose. By going the way of virtue instead of vice, he set himself up for mountains of hard work, pain, suffering, discomfort, difficulty. But he also paved the way for himself as a hero and future god—none of which would have been possible if he had shrunk away from challenge or given up when faced with adversity.

So, in reading the story of Hercules, we needn't feel sorry for him, and the constant attacks from Hera. Rather, these are trials that only strengthened the already-powerful Hercules. Rather than his adversity disrupting a life path that was "meant" to be easy and pleasurable, the struggle was the very *cause* of his later success and contentment. Hercules went along with his twelve labors willingly. That he did so can teach us a lot about ourselves, and our own (inner) demons.

Hercules teaches us first that a bad start in life doesn't have to be the end of the world. He truly had the cards stacked against him—he was the child of an affair and had someone out to kill him from the day of his birth. But he had other things in his favor, which he capitalized on: he was still a demi-god, and was raised to develop and strengthen his talents, despite his origins and difficulties. In Hercules' very nature we see the two potential paths: the option for the easier, more mediocre life or the chance at greatness, at godlike achievement and all the heroic deeds it would demand of him.

Hercules teaches us another lesson that is perhaps less common in modern times than it was in ancient Greece: life is hard. *Even when you're a half god*, life is still difficult, and dangerous, and uncomfortable, and chaotic. It doesn't matter that Hercules has superhuman strength—even he is tested to the limits of his abilities. So it doesn't really make a difference what gifts or advantages we possess; life will always push us to those limits, and demand we step up and be even better. These lessons, however, will never be easy. They will take grit and dedication, since they'll come in the form of struggle, disappointment, and challenge.

It's a matter of attitude. If we expect that *life should be easy*, we will be dismayed when it inevitably isn't. We will see the challenges that come our way as mistakes, or unwanted barriers in our path that should lead us directly and easily to the finish line. It's a perspective, in other words, that guarantees we will give up, lose faith, or resort to blame when we cannot achieve the things we want for ourselves. But if we acknowledge that life is not easy and never will be (and perhaps, that it shouldn't be!) then we can adopt the attitude of finding ways through and around troubles, with us coming out the other end strengthened and ennobled.

Nothing that is truly valuable is given for free. And in life, the best things of all are often those things that you've won and earned for yourself with blood, sweat and tears. There is never an easy way out. But knowing this, we can not only endure hardships but actually embrace them, grateful for the opportunity to test and prove ourselves, to dig deep and show ourselves what we're made of. Anyone can succeed in easy times. But it takes character and active effort to prove yourself in the hard times.

The success won in these hard times will be infinitely more valuable than reaching the end of an easy life with nothing much to show for it.

It's also important to remember that life's struggles never really go away. Hera never stops pursuing Hercules. She is taken as a fact of life. But, just like iron can be strengthened and made sharper in a forge of fire, or by being run along an even sharper sword, our adversities can sometimes be our training partners, the very force in life that challenges us to be better.

This force will *always* be there: we are on our path and suddenly, things don't go to plan. There's an obstacle in the road, an enemy, a misfortune or accident. And after that, there's another one! It is not the presence of these obstacles, but how we respond to them that will determine the quality of our success.

The easy path of avoiding troubles and seeking only pleasure may feel good in the moment, but it weakens a person. Willpower can be thought of as a muscle—when it's not exercised, it withers. The promise of a good, easy life is ultimately an illusion, because nothing is for free, and one way or another we pay for it. In forfeiting the challenge, in running away, avoiding hardship, blaming others or failing to rise to the challenge, we actually impoverish ourselves, and pass up a golden opportunity to become more than what we currently are.

The goddess Arete is the perfect personification of this idea—discipline, sacrifice, humble hard work and a virtuous life can seem plain and unexciting in the moment, but reap massive rewards later on. The flashy goddess Kakia promises a lot but is all talk—when it comes down to it, she is only offering a life of shame and pointlessness.

The easy life is nothing to be proud of, because it doesn't teach us anything, it doesn't inspire the best from us... in other words, it's "cheap" because it costs us nothing.

Sometimes we can look at amazing and accomplished figures and not see them for what they really are. We can envy those who are smarter, wealthier, more attractive or more talented, and want their life perhaps because we imagine that it's so much easier to be them!

But the truth is, *nobody* is spared hard work and difficulty in life, and in fact those that do well in life often experience *more* adversity, because they welcome it into their lives as a teacher. Hercules was naturally very strong—but his feats were never easy, never any less frightening or difficult than they would be for anyone else. In fact, we can be grateful that in comparison, our challenges are so much less daunting than poor Hercules'!

Many of the individuals in our book have faced difficulties that actually go beyond the normal lot of human suffering. These are the people who preach inner strength, commitment, hard work, discipline and all the rest—isn't it curious that those we consider most successful in these areas often actually faced more challenge and adversity than the average person? It makes you wonder how much this average person could achieve with their relatively small portion of troubles if they only adopted the attitude of Viktor Frankl, Thomas Edison, or Hercules.

Heroes (or "gods" of all kinds, both modern and ancient) have all the same fears and weaknesses, but the difference is that they don't allow their fear and weakness to be in the driving seat. The path is taken willingly. The feeling of valor, pride and satisfaction at the end of life is directly proportional to how much one was able to achieve in the face of hardship. There are no accolades awarded for taking the easy path, i.e. "big monsters, big prizes"! Each of us is half human, half god, since we have free will and possess the potentiality to be either exceptional or ordinary. Adversity is the arena where we prove to ourselves which aspect we will develop, which path we will go down.

Each of us is confronted by Kakia and Arete, by the choice to take the easy or the difficult route—sometimes several times a day! But instead of imagining that life has thrown you a curveball and been "unfair," look at your struggles for what they really are: invitations to be better.

Section Two. Masters from the Modern World

At this point in our book, we'll leave aside the great Greek myths and consider those stories we are likely to have a far deeper understanding of— those modern stories about remarkable people who have lived in our times, and faced challenge and adversity in such an impressive way that they take on their own mythical flavor.

The Greek myths certainly hold an archetypal heft that can be felt and understood in many cultures, but for the modern reader it may be necessary to turn to more local and contemporary heroes, who don't deal with jealous gods and demons, but with more familiar adversities like war, illness or personal injury.

If the antics of the mythical gods and goddesses hold no more curiosity for you than any other historical artifact, then you may appreciate similar tales of heroic feats of mortals who have lived in our times. Their acts of self-discipline, bravery, morality and good humor have given mankind a lesson in what's possible. The figures we'll consider next tell us as much about the human condition as the great titans and gods of old do, or perhaps more.

Viktor Frankl and creating self-meaning

We'll first turn our attention to the much-admired author Viktor Frankl, who could be said to have faced off with the god of death himself, only to emerge triumphant with a strengthened spirit and the will to survive and thrive, no matter the adversity.

His story is all the more inspiring because of how relatively ordinary it seems. Frankl was surely intelligent and privileged in some ways, but he also suffered immense hardships, the likes of which most people never experience in their lifetimes. In other words, he was human, and in being human he was able to inspire countless people all over the world to expand that definition in the most impressive ways possible.

Born in 1905, Frankl showed an interest in psychology from his earliest schooldays, and even maintained a correspondence with Freud for some time. He was curious about the inner drives of human beings—did they do what they did because they were seeking pleasure, or were people primarily motivated by the yearning for power and money?

Frankl was interested in this and more, and he studied psychology and philosophy, then medicine at the University of Vienna where he specialized in neurology and psychiatry. Though inspired by both Freud and Alfred Adler at the time, he soon came to challenge Freud's views that humans were driven by nothing more than primitive unconscious sexual and aggressive desires. He was also expelled from the Adler school for insisting that it was *meaning* that inspired man to think and behave as he did, rather than a striving for power.

Frankl's take on psychology was distinctly human, compared to what had come before it. He saw the prime motivator in human beings as the search and creation of meaning, blending themes from existentialist philosophy with humanist psychology. Frankl's vision of humanity was that we are driven on a profound level to live lives that make sense, that *mean* something, to us and in the grander scheme.

It was Frankl's own experience in the Nazi concentration camps, including Auschwitz, that gave him the opportunity to develop these ideas into what he ultimately christened *logotherapy*, a "third" Viennese school that challenged the two psychoanalytic conventions of the time. This approach was seemingly a more compassionate one that understood a person's health and well-being was not exclusively about meeting physical, social or security needs, but ultimately about the ability to create a meaningful life for oneself.

Based on his experiences, including those in the concentration camps, Frankl published thirty-nine books, with his *Man's Search for Meaning* capturing hearts and minds of readers all over the world to this day. The book has sold well past 10 million copies and has been translated into dozens of languages, proving that it speaks to people of all ages, nationalities and life circumstances.

The powerful thing is that Frankl wasn't merely hypothesizing—he actually lived his philosophy, and like a true hero, went into adversity and emerged stronger. Though his wife and children were killed in the camps, and though he witnessed depravity, despair and pain beyond what most of us can even imagine, he chose to use the experiences to cultivate a life philosophy of dignity, joy, strength and depth.

It's true that most of us will not experience a life as extreme as this, but nevertheless we can learn a lot from a man like Frankl who has been out to experience life's furthest reaches and come back to teach us how to tackle the more ordinary adversities of life. Let's take a closer look at what Frankl experienced, what he taught, and how we can use his lessons in our own lives.

In the camps, Frankl noticed that no matter how dire the situation was, there were always people who were kind to one another, sharing their last crumb of food with those who needed it more, or comforting and supporting others. This was proof for Frankl that beyond everything there still remained the option available to a person to *choose their own attitude*, no matter how bad their circumstances. How beautiful it must have seemed to Frankl, to contemplate that even in the face of death and despair, it was in the realm of possibility to *decide* to act with kindness, to smile, to hold on to what you believed in no matter how seriously it was threatened.

Concentration camp victims had everything taken from them—security, dignity, confidence, happiness, family, everything. Their heads were shaved, their families killed and their names forgotten. But what does a human *always* have, no matter what? No matter what, we always have the freedom to choose our own guiding values, to choose how we will respond to life.

This is a powerful message. Large groups underwent the same brutal treatment, and though some of them crumbled and lost hope, others became stronger. This proves to us that it's not the conditions of life per se that determine our success, but our attitudes toward these conditions—in other words, the meaning we ascribe to our own lives. It was the ability to seize and develop this divine human right to make our own meaning that Frankl came to understand as the key to a rich and fulfilled life.

What is different about Frankl's approach is that he doesn't deny the existence of suffering, or try to explain it away. He faced one of the most painful experiences a human being can undergo. Rather, his point was that ultimately, we always retain the right to define our experiences according to our own meaning, and we can choose love and compassion even in the face of others turning to death and destruction. We'll see this very theme repeated in some of the other figures we'll consider in later chapters.

If you're in the middle of adversity, it's tempting to rail against it, to get angry, to lose faith, to blame anything and everything, to give up. But Frankl reminds us that in troubles big and small, we always have the choice: how do *you* want to respond? What are your values, and how you will enact them? You can be faced with a cruel and unfair boss, a sudden accident or death of a loved one, a financial loss, a humiliation, or simply the daily irritations that trouble us all. But all the while, you are able to pause, look inside and choose your response. Always.

Nietzsche famously claimed, "Man can endure any how if only he has a why." Here is an important lesson, as Frankl sees it. Suffering is not a mistake or something to be avoided, but an integral part of human life that adds richness and depth to our time on this earth. After all, would Frankl's story have been as compelling without having spent those dark days imprisoned in the camps?

Suffering, then, is like an invitation to dig deep, to fire ourselves in the great forge of life and come out stronger. By choosing love, service to others, and meaningful work, we live well despite and even because of suffering. To put it simply, we all suffer, but it's our response to suffering that gives life its real meaning. We can tell ourselves a story about our suffering that inspires despair, hopelessness and blame. Or we can frame our suffering as fuel and use it to be better.

There are few successful people in the world who have lived a life free of suffering. The difference between those people and those who give up is that the former have taken charge of how that suffering is defined. Someone could fail in business, get divorced, lose loved ones or any number of setbacks, but emerge stronger, even claiming that the experience was a gift. If you are in the middle of adversity, look it square in the eye and ask it what it can teach you.

Of course, nobody is suggesting that it's a virtue to simply tolerate any maltreatment and never complain. But Frankl observed in the camps that those who survived and even thrived had something the others didn't—purpose. They had a strong, healthy connection to the world, whether that was someone they loved, a higher calling, unfinished work or a dream in the future they wanted to achieve. This teaches all of us the power of having faith in the universe at large, making plans for the future and trusting always that things can improve. Frankl even noticed that those who had lost hope seemed to literally die sooner than those fiercely holding on.

And it isn't only the values, meaning and purpose we have that matter, but how we manifest these qualities in the world. Frankl showed the strength of his character in *real life,* out "in the trenches" where his attitude was put to the test. Frankl explains, "We needed to stop asking about the meaning of life and instead think of ourselves as those who were being questioned by life—daily and hourly. Our answer must consist, not in talk and meditation, but in right action and right conduct. Life ultimately means taking the responsibility to find the right answers to its problems and to fulfill the tasks which it constantly sets for each individual."

This is a message that has real power. It's useless to dwell on abstracts and hypotheticals. We test our true grit in the arena of life itself, in our constant choices, actions, and speech. And those actions are most powerful when we choose kindness. Frankl discovered that there was kindness in some of his captors, and vicious cruelty in some of his fellow prisoners.

Beyond the groups and classifications we have for our fellow humans, there is a more fundamental difference: are we going to be people of compassion, gentleness and generosity? Or will we choose a darker path for ourselves? For Frankl, human beings either rise to the challenge to be good or they don't, but it has nothing to do with their religion, nationality, gender, or age.

Frankl's experience taught him to see the real depth and breadth of the human soul. Far beyond more simplistic conceptions of the human psyche being nothing more than a craving for sex or food or safety or control, Frankl challenged us to think more highly of ourselves, to demand kindness in the face of pain, to adopt a dignity not because it was easy, but precisely because it was difficult.

To follow in Frankl's footsteps, we don't need to pursue anything other than our heart and soul's deepest longing—to live a life of meaning and purpose. This is not something that can be done quickly, there are no hacks and tricks, and suffering is inevitably a part of the process. However, remember that others have gone before to light the way and show us another possibility. It can only benefit us to routinely look past the mundanities of life and tap into our deepest resource, our sense of *meaning*.

What is the legacy you wish to leave on this earth and why? What does your suffering mean? And even right now, in the most ordinary of moments, what can you do to truly elevate yourself and your experience? It's these questions that will lead down a path of the so called "well-lived life."

Marc Zupan and overcoming by doing

Though Viktor Frankl has passed away, he surely would have approved of Marc Zupan, whose autobiography title tells you everything you need to know about him: *GIMP : When Life Deals You a Crappy Hand, You Can Fold—or You Can Play.* Zupan, too, showed how your true character shines through not when everything is going right for you, but when trouble hits and you're forced to make the best of it. Zupan is certainly not the only sportsman to make lemonade out of the lemons life gave him, but he is one of the more well known.

One night in 1993, Zupan got drunk with teammates at a bar after a game of soccer, and climbed into the back of a truck belonging to his friend. This friend set off—driving drunk—and when he had an accident, threw the sleeping Zupan out of the vehicle into a canal where he clung for dear life to a branch for an incredible fourteen hours. He was eventually rescued by a passerby, but the ordeal left him almost completely paralyzed, able to only walk short distances with crutches, and bound to a wheelchair for life.

For an athlete and sportsman like Zupan, this could only have felt like a death sentence. Used to enjoying and using his bodily strength to the fullest, he was now weakened and unable to play the sport he loved. Or was he?

Zupan arguably achieved his real success only *after* his accident. He kept playing rugby, but from his wheelchair. He was a quad rugby national champion, and the quad rugby player of the year in 2004. His team won bronze at the 2004 Summer Paralympics and gold at the 2008 games. His team, "Superman's Crip-Tonite," came second in the Red Bull Flugtag in Texas, the name proving that Zupan fully intended to treat his "disability" with irreverence and good humor.

Beyond that, Zupan has made a name for himself as a media personality that many people look up to. He's given interviews and appeared on shows and TV series, as well as in guest roles in all kinds of productions, including the *Murderball* movie. He's visited the White House, and done other impressive feats like rock climbing and skydiving.

Though he must have felt utter despair hanging from a tree that night, Zupan no longer looks at the accident as a tragedy. When asked in an interview whether he wished it never happened, he replied, "No, I don't think so. My injury has led me to opportunities and experiences and friendships I would never have had before. And it has taught me about myself. In some ways, it's the best thing that ever happened to me."

Zupan's no-nonsense attitude and refusal to let a moment of adversity determine his entire life make him an endearing character. There's a lot we can learn from him—hopefully without having to go through the same sort of ordeal! Like the Buddhist farmer in our earlier chapter, we see that Zupan had the wisdom to look at the seemingly disastrous events in his life without pre-judgment. He might certainly have felt wretched at some points, but ultimately, he decided not to go with the story, *My life is ruined, I can't do anything now, I'm a victim of a stupid and senseless accident…*

Though Zupan's story is a thoroughly modern one, we can't help but detect the grandeur of a hero's arc, seeing the athlete struck by the "gods" but ready to bravely battle his demons to emerge triumphant. The trick is, however, that this athlete's success did not take the form he expected it to. That fateful night, it would seem that all the young man's dreams were robbed from him—but he simply went on to create different dreams!

It's truly a marvelous thing when someone achieves their grandest visions for their life, not despite their challenges, but even because of them. Zupan took the hand he'd been dealt and ran with it. Sure, he could never play the sport as he knew it again. But so what? In a Herculean (a significant word choice, considering our previous discussion) act of bravery, creativity, and determination, he did what he could—and he did it extremely well. Zupan's story teaches us that it doesn't really matter what the details and circumstances of your life are. What matters is your attitude, your values, your goals and how hard you're willing to work to achieve them.

If Zupan felt despair at having the door forever closed on a certain version of his life, he never allowed it to stop him, or interfere with him asking what new shape his life would take. An excellent antidote to adversity is not to hunker down and endure it, but to *reframe* it entirely, even to the extent that it no longer resembles adversity at all. With a little flexibility of spirit, imagination, and the guts to "accept what you can't change and change what you can't accept," Zupan hit it out the park.

Many of us cling to a story of ourselves as a victim. We get bogged down by the question of whether something is "fair" or not, or we get lost in blame and anger at others. We never even realize how much of this narrative is purely optional! While it may be true that people are sometimes struck by accident, or treated unfairly, or lose out for no good reason, it's also true that these things are not strictly the end of the world—and Zupan proves it.

The startling difference in his attitude is one of agency—he looks at what he wants, and what he can do to get it. Simple. "One door closes and another opens," as they say, and dwelling on the door that's closed could cause you to not notice all the other doors that are now open to you. The essence of this story is to be found all over: the businessman whose "failed" invention turns out to have an alternate use and becomes a raging success. The woman who feels like her cancer scare has given her a new lease on life. Any number of people who look back on past crises and wistfully think that, in hindsight, it was precisely what needed to happen to them at that moment.

How can we inject a little of Marc Zupan's pluck and fearlessness into our own lives? We don't have to wait until some disaster befalls us. Much like Viktor Frankl suggests, it's all a question of attitude. The next time things don't go your way, pause for a moment and resist jumping in to frame the experience as a Bad Thing. Instead of looking at how things *were*, turn your attention to the present and the future: what else is possible now? Yes, you've lost your job, but doesn't that also mean you're now free to get a better one? Falling seriously ill can shake your faith and make you see the worst in others, but it can also be a golden opportunity to do something really special with the time you have left—what could that be?

It's a given that life will seldom go according to plan. If we want to be the kind of people who look back and call their suffering a "blessing in disguise," we have to be willing to let go of certain fixed ideas or assumptions about ourselves, our lives, what we want, what we're capable of. When life is progressing as expected, we pull back from taking chances out of fear, believing we can't do certain things.

Isn't it wonderful then, when life steps in, takes the choice away from you and puts you in precisely the situation that will prove to you that you're very much stronger than you thought you were? We have to have the openness, the bravery and flexibility to rechristen tragedies as opportunities, or failures as valuable lessons. Knowing that pain and disaster *will* happen in some measure in everyone's life, what's the best attitude we can take when it rears its head?

Before life forces your hand and sends you, willing or not, into a "dark night of the soul," do some soul-searching yourself. Look very closely at the stories you tell yourself. Marc Zupan might have told himself, "I'm an athlete and sportsman. My life has no meaning without that, without my body," and that story would certainly have been damaging to him after his accident. But he instead told himself the story, "I'm Marc and I don't give up, I find a way, no matter what, and I have a damn good time doing it," and his experience was completely different! It's not the adversity that changes, but the response to it. In this way, we can all transform adversity, disaster, failure, humiliation and loss into the best lessons of our lives.

It's this attitude that allows us to see the hidden value in suffering, and the immense power we all possess to define our own experience. If your small business fails and you lose your life's savings, you could yell at the sky, blame everyone else, become bitter and never take another chance again. Or, you could experience something wonderful: that even when you're flat broke you're still alive, still you, and can still make more plans, can still have hope, can still do good in the world. Brilliant! People sometimes say that they're glad for challenge in life because, if nothing else, it allows them to prove to themselves that they *can* survive, that they're made of tough stuff, and that it's not really the end of the world to lose, to hurt, to make a mistake.

Perhaps we can take most inspiration simply from Zupan's sense of humor. He uses words for himself (like "crip" or "gimp") that could have easily hurt and offended him, but he decided instead to laugh at himself first. In doing so, he took away the power—for him or anybody else—to mock him or put him down. This attitude may seem flippant but really shows a deep confidence. Rather than shrinking from his flaws, limitations or disabilities, he looked at them directly, shrugged and thought, *So what?*

We could all stand to drop a fragile ego if it stands in the way of us simply living.

The next time you fail, try it: quickly and completely own your mistake, laugh at yourself and move on. So what if you've been a complete idiot? Isn't it so much more freeing to acknowledge and own a mistake than letting it define you?

Jean-Dominique Bauby and the value of time

In the earlier part of this book, we saw that out of Pandora's box came all the evils of the world. This was Zeus's "gift" to the wise, beautiful girl who had everything already. In the story, it was meant to be an act of revenge, but in both Frankl's and Zupan's case, the "evil" was really a powerful force for *good* in their lives, one way or another. It's curious how many people who've experienced profound loss and change would have it no other way—and they certainly wouldn't choose to go back and live a more mediocre life!

Jean-Dominique Bauby is another example, and you may already be familiar with his story if you've watched the movie *The Diving Bell and the Butterfly,* or read the book that inspired it. At the young age of forty-three, Bauby experienced what many of us have only glimpsed in our nightmares: he suffered a stroke and fell into a coma that left him, twenty days later, utterly unable to speak, or to move his arms or legs. He could not even move his mouth.

Can you imagine the horror of waking up to a life so profoundly changed? We can only guess at the shock Bauby must have felt to have lived a full and normal life one moment, only to wake up less than a month later to a new prison—his own body. Inside, his mind worked the same as it ever had, and he could sense the world as always. The only difference was that he couldn't express himself, couldn't talk, couldn't ask for anything. It was as though he no longer had any way to reach and connect with the world outside him. Couldn't express his pain. Couldn't ask a question. Couldn't tell his two young children that he loved them.

But there was one thing he *could* do—blink. And, just like Zupan had done, he decided not to despair over what he couldn't do, but capitalize on what he could. Bauby was a journalist by trade, and edited the French fashion magazine *Elle* at the time.

Words were his living. Remarkably, Bauby, with the help of those around him, found a way to communicate with others through blinking alone. An associate would read out loud the letters of the alphabet and Bauby would blink when he reached the letter he wanted. Then the alphabet would be read again and so each letter, each word and sentence was painstakingly put together through the only channel left open to Bauby—the tiny movements of his eyelids.

In the many hours he spent alone and in bed, Bauby had only his imagination to keep him company, and in time composed a book that he would then "dictate" to his friend Claude Mendibil, who'd then write it out for him. Adapting as he went, Mendibil learnt to start with those letters most frequent in the French language to speed things up. Being an editor, and having time on his hands, Bauby took pains to create a book inspired by his experiences. Bauby had always had a way with words. But it must have been overwhelming to know the cost and effort it took to express a single letter—no doubt Bauby quickly found ways to become an even more concise and impactful writer!

The book, an autobiography of his life and experience with "locked-in syndrome," was an enormous success. Sadly, Bauby died just two days after the book was published, and never knew its success. He died at age forty-four from sudden complications from pneumonia. Later a short documentary film was made about him, and then in 2007 the rights to his autobiography were acquired for the major motion picture with the same name.

Although close friends criticized some parts of the story's depiction of him and his partner, the movie nevertheless touched many people, and the consensus was that the film told a difficult story in a gentle and beautiful way.

What can we learn from Bauby? Perhaps you're immediately struck by the sheer amount of hard work it must have taken to "write" the book. While most of us take our ordinary capabilities for granted, Bauby had to work with the most meager of tools. How many times have we put off doing a task that someone less fortunate would relish simply having the opportunity to complete? There are people in the world who can easily write, and have the talent to do so, and yet never have the courage, self-discipline or faith to actually attempt it.

On the most superficial level, Bauby's tale is a lesson in patient diligence. Every book, not just his, is written a single letter at a time. Granted, he took a longer time to write each letter, but he did it, one step at a time. The next time you're feeling overwhelmed by the enormity of a task ahead of you, remember that your task, just like Bauby's, is merely composed of tiny little steps. You don't have to work miracles—you just have to do one step. And then when you're done, do the next one.

But Bauby's story is remarkable not just for the effort he put into writing a book. Internally, he must have dreamt up a million possible scenarios to add to his autobiography, a million metaphors or anecdotes or stories. The trouble was, he couldn't waste too much time. Bauby was ill and would get tired quickly, over and above the grueling work of picking through letter after letter. He must have realized quickly: he needed to be concise.

The fact is, however, that none of us has endless time at our disposal. We may *think* we have a lot of time, but so did Bauby, before he was hit with a stroke from out of the blue. Even after his tragic stroke, he only lived two more years, and on some profound level he must have understood just how brief his time was, and how urgent it was to say what he needed to say before it was too late.

Self-discipline is an invaluable skill to learn not simply because it makes you more effective, and gives you a greater chance at reaching the goals you truly want for yourself. Self-discipline is valuable because it helps us *cut to the chase*. To put it bluntly, we don't have all the time in the world.

Do we want to waste the opportunities we have on things we don't care about? Or do we want to do our very best with the precious time we have, right here and right now? When you frame things this way, self-discipline is not so much about being strict with yourself, but *valuing* yourself—valuing the talents, opportunities, time and life you've been given. Bauby chose to use what time he had left wisely.

In Bauby's book, Mithra-Grandchamp is a racehorse that signifies the idea of missed opportunity. The horse was meant to win a race, and Bauby and a friend intended to bet on him, but got distracted and failed to make their bets in time. Mithra-Grandchamp won the race, and they realized how much money they could have potentially made but didn't. In the book he writes,

"The memory of that event has only just come back to me, now doubly painful: regret for a vanished past and, above all, remorse for lost opportunities. Mithra-Grandchamp is the women we were unable to love, the chances we failed to seize, the moments of happiness we allowed to drift away. Today it seems to me that my whole life was nothing but a string of those small near misses: a race whose result we know beforehand but in which we fail to bet on the winner."

How many of our own racehorses have we let zoom by us, mistakenly thinking that there will always be another one? Can any of us say that we've lived a life that will leave us with no regrets should we find ourselves on our deathbeds with time to think it all over? If today was your last day, would you have felt you'd wasted it, in hindsight? Perhaps all we can do is to constantly have the self-discipline to remind ourselves that we are not so different from Bauby.

He asks elsewhere in the book, "Does it take the harsh light of disaster to show a person's true nature?" We can take this question as a direct challenge to us as readers. Can we seize life and make the best of it without having to undergo the ordeal that Bauby did? It's easy to agree that "you only appreciate it when it's gone" but can we actually *act*, today, as though that were true? Self-discipline can be hard if all it is is hard work. But if it's fired up from within, motivated by a deeper hunger for something you deeply understand to be finite—perhaps these are the conditions that inspire sincere action.

These are difficult things to think about, when our own mortality is not plainly staring us in the face. But we can always stop, take a moment and ask ourselves whether our thoughts, actions and words are wasting what we have, or making the best use of it. When facing a decision, it may be easier to let go of fear if you know that the regret of not acting will be so much more difficult to bear.

However, none of this is cause for hopelessness. Like Zupan, Bauby had an attitude that was refreshingly lighthearted. He didn't wallow in self-pity, or frame himself as some tragic hero caught in a dreadful trap. When he felt alone or afraid or exhausted, he didn't deny it, only accepted it gently, even trying to turn it into something beautiful, something poetic that others might read and feel within themselves. In this way, suffering was not a problem, per se, but merely a part of life, and life itself was so cherished, that the negative parts of it didn't matter.

The fact that Bauby died so soon after the publication of his book is highly suggestive. The mind is a powerful thing and we can't know if Bauby consciously left this world, satisfied that he had done what he needed to. In some ways, this is a tragic outcome. But in others, isn't it inspiring how much can be done in a mere two years, if that's what it comes to?

Bauby was forced to be still and to be silent, but he used this time to create. Though his body failed and he had very little means to communicate, he only ramped up his efforts to share what was in his heart with the world. There was no need to feel bitter, to curse life or go on a maudlin, self-involved journey about the "meaning of life"—rather, Bauby took the facts of his circumstances as they were, and showed us how to bear them with good-natured grace.

There are many ways for life to not go to plan, but there are also many ways to be brave, and many gifts to be had, if we know how to look.

Thomas Edison and the pursuit of failure

Who is Thomas Edison? Almost everyone knows him as more or less the most famous inventor who ever lived. Not only is he known for the invention of the lightbulb, the phonograph, the Quadruplex telegraph and the motion picture camera, he currently holds more than a thousand other patents in the United States. It's hard to imagine, with this illustrious resume, how Edison could have been anything other than a success all throughout life.

And yet, he wasn't. Today, the story of Thomas Edison is seen as one of unimaginable success, but in reality, it was almost equal parts adversity. Edison suffered a vicious bout of scarlet fever as a child, and the damage it did to his hearing stayed with him for the rest of his life—as an adult he eventually lost hearing entirely in one ear and retained very little in the other.

Edison had humble beginnings, and was a hyperactive, easily distracted child whom teachers found difficult and even too stupid to learn anything. As a child he never stayed in school for long and was largely homeschooled, making money here and there selling sweets, fruit and newspapers, and embarking on many small entrepreneurial ventures. Edison was a true autodidact, and was driven by a curiosity to understand and a desire to improve people's lives using technology and common sense. He was a telegraph operator in his teens, often working at night, and was already experiencing limitations due to his hearing loss. He was a curious and voracious reader, however, and constantly designing and inventing things.

Edison was fired from his first two jobs very quickly. His first real invention was the electric vote recorder. It failed. He kept at it and eventually the device was manufactured on a large scale, after countless improvements to the design. Edison married and had children, and soon had his own lab at his disposal, where he and his other "muckers" invented the famous phonograph to record a voice and play it back. Then came the incandescent lightbulb and fluorescent light—and the countless nights in electrical experimentation, endless experiments, endless failures.

Edison was never without a project in the works, and usually dozens were on the go at one time. Once he succeeded in something, he worked to improve it. He designed, built, and tested new devices and then tried to get them manufactured and sold all over the world.

He worked on X-rays, storage batteries, in mining and chemical engineering, electricity and even the design of a talking doll. He improved the telephone for Western Union and refined many other inventors' work. Edison, by now well-known and admired for his genius and incredible work ethic, had a normal-sized ego and was fond of putting his success down to nothing more than the willingness to work.

"Opportunity is missed by most people because it comes wearing overalls and looks like work," Edison famously said. He was not a man to boast about his intellect or natural talent (like our mythical Arachne!) but rather understood that what mattered was what you *did*, and that took hard work and persistence.

Many of the famous quotes now attributed to Edison speak to his attitude toward creating: "Just because something doesn't do what you planned it to do, doesn't mean it's useless." Could there be any more of a quintessential inventor's manifesto as that? Edison was curious by nature, and saw opportunity all around him. He didn't get bogged down in labeling some things "success" and others "failures."

He merely maintained the open mind of a rational scientist and observed. What happened when he did X, Y and Z? What happened if he changed a little and tried again? What could he learn, and how could he test this updated hypothesis?

Edison is the man credited with saying he didn't discover the lightbulb, but a thousand ways *not* to make a lightbulb. This lighthearted joke conceals a deep insight: that the most resilient attitude in life is often the most flexible one, because flexibility allows one to look in many different ways, to seek out the "blessing in disguise."

We can follow Einstein's example when we let go of old narratives about how things *should* be, and when we stop expecting our success to take only a very limited shape, or else we classify it a failure.

This is what psychologists have now come to understand as a "growth mindset." Rather than seeing ourselves as fixed entities, with stable sets of skills and abilities and a personality that is largely settled, we can understand that we are always, always growing—if we allow it. With this growth mindset, we don't see "failure" as a threat to our identity, or worth. We expect failure because we understand it's part and parcel of the process of growth—which is what we are primarily interested in.

A scientist is interested in the outcome of his experiment, whatever it is. This is because no matter what shape it takes, he gains in knowledge. In valuing this knowledge, he continues to experiment, grateful for every second he gets to learn and develop, to challenge himself intellectually. To gain ground, he must be patient, think clearly, make good plans, test them, and never stop improving. You'll notice that nowhere in that process is an ego required!

In fact, vanity can only get in the way of discovery and invention of all kinds. A "fixed mindset" can give us a mental concept of ourselves as successful only if and when we succeed—so what will happen when we fail? We'll translate the event into a personal flaw, feel bad about it, and even shrink away from trying again because the blow to our confidence was unbearable. Rather than trying and failing, we choose not to try at all, or limit ourselves to only those activities we can be sure of performing well.

But a person with a growth mindset doesn't mind what lies on the path to the goal. They don't see failure as a problem—they may scarcely even see it as a failure to start with. Something may not go as planned, but they'll look at it and even feel grateful, knowing that they are still one step closer to their goal.

They know that learning is sometimes messy, and they are not embarrassed to make a mistake, go the wrong path or have everything blow up in their faces. Embracing the fact that growth is a process, they intrinsically understand that there is a path to walk, and that path could well entail some twists and turns on the way.

When Edison began his life, he had no idea that he would one day be called "the world's greatest inventor." Earning that accolade was not his goal, either. He was unknown as an inventor for very many years before he started to achieve success and fame. Before this, he was just like any one of us, working away at the things we care about, failing occasionally, succeeding occasionally. Edison himself never had any certainty that *anything* he did would succeed—and yet he still persisted.

What we can learn from Edison is to do the same, not at some end point where we know the path we took was the right one, but right now, where we're still unsure about how things work, or what we need to do. Edison teaches us quite simply not to give up.

Try again. You'll have days when you feel your task is impossible. Keep trying. You'll even have days where you feel like you're going backwards—keep trying still. Learn from your mistakes and make better mistakes the next time round. Though successful people have succeeded far more often than the ordinary person, they've also failed far more often!

Edison did not believe in luck or genius or accident. He believed in honest work, period. Use what you have at your disposal and "hustle while you wait" rather than expecting that everything will come together in the future, or be handed to you if only you're deserving enough. Take ego, morality and emotion out of the equation—set your goal in front of you and decide on the steps you need to take to achieve it.

And then, find out exactly what you need to do to convert whatever talents and opportunities you have into something you can be proud of.

Easier said than done, of course, and nobody would suggest that we all need to strive to be prolific inventors. So far we've looked at athletes, authors and now a scientist, but what if you're none of these? What if you don't aim for wealth or fame? Edison still teaches us that we can always achieve the best of *our* potential, and make a life that is worth living *on our own terms.*

Edison excelled in the sciences, but he never achieved a thing as a writer and likely couldn't dance, paint, be a politician or cater a meal for five hundred people. But he found the way to make the best use of the personal talents he did possess, and today it scarcely matters that some of his schoolteachers found his handwriting unsatisfactory, or that there are people who can swim better than he can.

Edison invented because he was an inventor. It was not a passion so much as a way of life, something he almost couldn't help but do. Can we learn to bravely pursue our own talents and interests the way he did? Try to think of what you're most passionate and curious about in this world—about those things that have always held your love and fascination, even as a child. Think of those things you pursued with energy and diligence, even though they didn't make you any money, and even though you didn't strictly need to do them. Dedicating your life to a particular path can seem daunting—but not if what you are pursuing is genuinely the thing that interests you most in life.

So many of us limit ourselves artificially. We tell ourselves stories about why we can't achieve, why we shouldn't even try. We may believe fervently in a vision of our identity that is purely fictional, but which nevertheless becomes a self-fulfilling prophesy. We might say, "Sure, that's fine for that person, but that could never happen for *me*" or "I'm just an unlucky person. I'll never be successful."

When you can set aside these stories, limitations, assumptions, expectations... then you can see the world as it is, with all its rich possibilities and avenues to explore. An inventor knows this instinctively—that there is always a way, always a solution. Can't see it yet? It doesn't mean it doesn't exist, it just means you haven't found it yet, that's all. If you try something and it doesn't work, well, there's another avenue to explore.

Finally, Edison can teach us a lot about creativity. Self-discipline and creativity are not opposites. If we can have the self-discipline to routinely make time and space for it, our imagination and creativity can flourish fully. Clear your head and open your mind so your God-given creativity can do its magic. Look at things from another perspective, be bold, ask strange questions and don't be afraid to find out the answers... And before you decide to give up, ask yourself whether you've really exhausted all possibilities. Ask for help or take a break—it doesn't matter how slow you walk, only that you don't stop walking!

Sir James Dyson and the decision of perseverance

So great is English businessman and inventor Sir James Dyson's success that you probably already know what he is famous for, simply by his name. Dyson vacuum cleaners are considered the gold standard all over the world, and people like and trust this brand more than any other. But this great empire took time to build, and it started with nothing more than Dyson getting frustrated with his own Hoover vacuum cleaner—it always lost suction power and replacing its disposable bags was a chore.

It might be a simple thing to say that Dyson went on to create the world's first bagless vacuum cleaner using the idea of cyclonic separation, but this conceals how epic a journey it really was—it took a whopping *5126 failures* for Dyson to get the invention just right. And that was just the beginning. Even when he had designed a product he knew was superior in so many ways, the fact was that the disposable vacuum bag market was a million-pound industry and he faced immense push-back in trying to market and sell his invention.

No distributors wanted to go against the grain, and the market was unwilling to budge. People liked and knew Hoover cleaners, and that was that. But, perhaps taking a page out of Edison's book, Dyson pushed on and tried to find something that *would* work. He marketed a bright pink version of his new Dyson vacuum cleaner in Japan in 1983, where it won an award. From there he was able to get a patent for the design in the United States. *Still*, he faced resistance in the UK.

But where there wasn't a way, Dyson attempted to make one. Instead of giving up, he decided he'd have to make his own company. At the age of forty-six he embarked on producing and marketing the product himself. You can already guess how the rest of the story went—Dyson built that company up, and today it's valued at almost $4 billion. Like Edison, he was tireless in his work and never allowed adversity to stop him.

But Dyson displayed a truly rare singlemindedness. The next time you look at a Dyson vacuum cleaner, you can imagine it as a symbol of rock-solid perseverance. Dyson pushed through frightening debt, discouragement from his peers and immense resistance from the market.

So, what could a vacuum cleaner magnate teach us about personal discipline?

Dyson is, if anything, an expert on failure. Rather than trying to avoid it at all costs, he now actively seeks it out, knowing how valuable it is in the creation and innovation process—he even spends several million pounds every week on research and design, i.e. the pursuit of failing, learning and trying again, or what he calls *educative failure.*

"Stumbling upon the next great invention in an 'ah-hah!' moment is a myth," Dyson says. "It is only by learning from mistakes that progress is made...each failure brought me closer to solving a problem." What does failing give you? Insight and experience. It tells you what doesn't work, and maybe even why. Failing is a lesson, if we can learn to embrace it.

Imagine a forty-two-year-old Dyson with money problems, bad debt, literally thousands of failed prototypes under his belt and a market that didn't want what he had to sell. It's easy to think of the countless people who would have given up in such circumstances. But Dyson did not. He had confidence in his ideas, and the courage to keep on even when others didn't share his vision. The incredible thing is that Dyson achieved after so long, and more than that, *he kept going* even after he'd found some success.

His perseverance was not just a way to overcome adversity and come out the other end. It was a way of life. Today his company thrives on open-mindedness, bravery, and courage. He has claimed to love hiring younger people who are unburdened with expectations of how things "should" be done, and are more fearless when it comes to trying something completely new. Here we see the growth mindset appearing again: by putting ourselves in the frame of eternal students, we never allow ourselves to become complacent, or assume we know all the answers.

If we can comfortably tolerate the unknown, we can give ourselves a real chance of actually grasping it and doing things that haven't been done before.

In the end, it's not quite *what* Dyson did as *how* he did it. There must have surely been times when he doubted himself and was tired, and just wanted to give up. Undoubtedly his work took an enormous amount of effort and diligence and, you guessed it, self-discipline. We often think of self-discipline only as the skill it takes to push through and work hard even when we're lazy or tired or unmotivated. But it's more than this.

Self-discipline is the ability to drive ourselves forward when *everything* else is threatening that progress, or when we don't even know the direction we're supposed to be going in. Self-discipline is about the habit of looking plainly at your fear, every day, and realizing it will never go away, and that if you want to achieve your goals, you're going to have to *act despite that fear.*

When asked, Dyson tells his admirers that he never gives advice, and that we shouldn't listen to advice. He even warns against doing market research because it so often takes the wind out of your sails. He believes people shouldn't strive to be entrepreneurs in the first place—rather, identify what you care about and go at it full throttle. The success will come when it comes, but in the meantime, your work is always here, in the present, being the best you can be no matter what.

Like so many ultra-accomplished businessmen of his caliber, he ironically doesn't think of himself as one, and likely wouldn't have found the same success if his primary goal was to win fame and make a lot of money. This gives us a clue to the correct attitude toward success. Those who make it work are masters at the *process*, and they are not overly attached to the outcome. This is the growth mindset applied to business. If your ego and vanity shackle you to an idea of how your success should look, you'll be less resilient in the face of adversity, and less wiling to learn when life doesn't go to plan. The greatest people are often far more comfortable with complete failure and even humiliation than those who have their eye set on fame and glory at the finish line.

These lessons are not just for business. Any time we want to improve, learn, create something new or gain mastery or knowledge, we must work for it. Just like Jean-Dominique Bauby was able to write a bestseller with *less* physical capacity than most people, it's sobering to think that Dyson was successful even with far more resistance and difficulty than the average person can expect in their endeavors. The next time you look at the limits and obstacles in your way, ask yourself if they're really preventing you from doing what you want... or if it's *you* and the beliefs you hold that are keeping you back.

This is an exercise in recalibration. For whatever reason, some of us may believe that life ought to be far easier than it is, and take any sign of discomfort, adversity or unpleasantness as a sure sign that we're on the wrong path, and should just quit. Anybody can dream about the wonderful goals they'd love to have for themselves, but the more decisive factor is how much discomfort and uncertainty you're able to withstand, not how big and fanciful you can make your dreams.

Anyone could say, "It would be great to be a wealthy and successful businessman," but the rubber hits the road when you realize that this path is one of constantly facing your fears and working incredibly hard.

Dyson perhaps possessed an almost supernatural talent for persevering despite all odds, and many would correctly say it's survivor bias to claim that his perseverance was a good thing—would we have admired him so much if he had failed all his life, and never made anything of his business? Nobody can predict the future, and there's no saying what fate or luck will land in our laps. But for someone like Dyson, this is irrelevant.

Maintaining an unflappable attitude and a pride in one's work—whether it's successful or not—is what will keep you persevering, in the absence of external reward, praise or anything else. Like the other people we've explored in this book, Dyson found a source of his own value and meaning—and it came from within. Only by having a fearsome *inner* drive can we keep going no matter what the circumstances. When we believe in ourselves, are well aligned to our values and care about the process rather than the outcome, then we can simply take failures along the way in stride.

It may be a helpful practice to *joyfully welcome* failure when it happens to you. Literally smile and celebrate when things flop, fail or turn out completely differently than you'd hoped for. It's proof that you're growing. Thank the universe for giving you a great clue, and a wonderful gift on your endless journey. Don't give your ego the chance to realize it's been bruised. Laugh at yourself if you must, and swiftly move along. Rather than turning away in embarrassment at what's been done "wrong," simply become curious like Edison and study the problem itself: Why did it happen this way? What could you do better next time? How are you going to make that happen? Identifying the very next step to get you back in the game can be a wonderful antidote to feeling demoralized at a setback.

This doesn't only apply to inventions dreamt up in a laboratory. We all make grand plans for ourselves that crash and burn. Our dream job isn't what we thought it would be, we bought something foolish, said the wrong thing, broke something valuable, mismanaged a social matter, injured our knee while running or discovered our souffle keeps getting a dent in the middle no matter what we do.

But it's OK to fail, it's OK to change course midway, and it's OK to start all over again and try something really outrageous. Provided your mistakes don't literally threaten lives, why shouldn't you take the opportunity to try as many things as you can? Why shouldn't you use your entire life as a laboratory, and test out what works and what doesn't?

To practice some of this in your own life, start changing the way you talk about failure. A good start is to remove the word from your vocabulary entirely! Instead of saying you failed, reframe it: you got a different result from the one you were expecting. This small tweak can lead to large mental shifts around the way you think about learning, work and failure. Make a point of voluntarily sharing all the times you've made a mistake. Be honest and straightforward—isn't it a relief, in some ways, to just accept that things aren't perfect the first time round?

If someone calls you out on an error or criticizes your work, thank them. It takes a deep confidence and sense of security to know that being wrong doesn't threaten your sense of self-worth, and isn't something to deny or get defensive about. Rather than seeing a mistake or failure as life slapping you in the face, start to think of it as a kind teacher who is constantly working to keep you on your toes, to help you evolve and develop. If you are comfortable looking at, talking about and experiencing feelings of failure, you become in a sense immune to them. You realize how little power failing has over you.

You failed. So what? What's more, you'll fail *again*. So what? A great insight can come when you realize that people will often only judge your mistakes harshly if *you* do so first. If you can look at your life without shame or regret or embarrassment, very few other people will be tempted to do so. If your attitude is to never be ashamed of the results of hard work and curiosity, why should anyone else?

Stephen King and the defeat of judgment, rejection, and criticism

Stephen King's story of failure is now so well-known to other writers that it's taken on the quality of a myth itself—like the twelve impossibly heroic tasks assigned to Hercules. The story goes that King's first novel to be published, *Carrie*, was rejected thirty times before finally making it, and the rest, as they say, is history.

King today has published sixty-one novels and two hundred short stories, and several of his best loved works have been made into films, comics and TV series, including *The Shining, It, Pet*

Sematary, and many more. Today, even those completely unfamiliar with the horror/thriller genre will recognize his work. He's won the Bram Stoker Award, British Fantasy Society Award, World Fantasy Award, the Medal for Distinguished Contribution to American Letters, the National Medal of Arts and the O. Henry Award, to name a few.

But in the beginning, King was just an unknown writer with a passion for writing. With *Carrie*, even he himself got fed up and threw the manuscript in the bin; it was his wife Tabitha who fished it out and made him persevere. Thus started a literary career that only went from strength to strength. King has even gone on to write popular books and articles for writers, talking about his life, his process, and his trials and tribulations as a creator.

He's said to have literally hung up every single rejection letter received from a publishing house on the wall of his office. He claims that seeing them there doesn't demoralize him, but eggs him on to do better, to persevere. And it paid off! Stephen King is today a household name and one of the richest novelists in the world, with a net worth of almost half a billion dollars. His books have sold more than 350 million copies internationally.

According to King, "Talent is cheaper than table salt. What separates the talented individual from the successful one is a lot of hard work." Sound familiar? We can imagine Jean-Dominique Bauby or Edison or Marc Zupan saying the same thing. King is no starving artist who decides to put pen to paper only when the spirit moves him, or when he's feeling inspired. Instead, he's taken a very practical, no-nonsense and humble approach to the making of art—just do it.

King does not believe that artists should try to work other jobs to support their art, but rather that it is art that gives nourishment to life, and creativity should be prioritized. This means that anyone who takes the artistic life seriously must actively pursue it, and have the self-discipline to push back against fear, laziness, distraction or lack of motivation.

It's fitting that the horror writer has had fear so centrally at the core of his life's work. The author, like so many others, suffered from sometimes cripplingly low self-confidence in his work, doubt about his talent, and even the temptation to give up and do something easier. Every aspiring writer knows that the "inner critic" can be so relentless and painful that they would rather avoid creating at all for fear of being judged, rejected or criticized.

But isn't it refreshing to know that even one of the most successful authors of our time not only failed occasionally, but failed often, even extravagantly? For some authors (or artists of any kind) criticism can be incredibly difficult to take. It shrivels the ego and demolishes confidence. You could find yourself asking, "Who am I to think that I have something to say? Or something to create? Why should anybody listen to me?" But perhaps King's success comes down to adopting the right attitude to this rejection.

"I have spent a good many years since—too many, I think—being ashamed about what I write. I think I was forty before I realized that almost every writer of fiction or poetry who has ever published a line has been accused by someone of wasting his or her God-given talent. If you write (or paint or dance or sculpt or sing, I suppose), someone will try to make you feel lousy about it, that's all."

King doesn't have an explanation for this. Who knows why people tear one another down, or judge or criticize? In any case, it doesn't matter. The existence of criticism is simply to be regarded as a fact of life, and accepted along with any other natural law. The trick is not to give rejection too much authority over you. This is true for a writer especially, but applies to anyone who creates, builds, performs, designs or offers something for public consumption.

It can be so easy to assume that people who claim you're bad *are right*. But who's to say? The only one who can ultimately decide on our self-worth is ourselves. The thirty rejections that King received on *Carrie*—were they because his book was objectively worthless? If King had thought so (or rather, if his wife had thought so), the book would have remained in the trash and everyone would have assumed that yes, it was unfit for publication.

Many, many talented people have been dissuaded from expressing themselves, saying what they need to or using their talents to their fullest solely because they fear the judgment and rejection of others. What an enormous waste! Think of all the many stories the world would not have gotten to appreciate had King thrown in the towel and decided that he wasn't good enough, and not worth listening to.

But we do the same to ourselves and our dreams and talents every time we take rejection personally and decide to withdraw from life as a result. Whether it's in artistic criticism, whether it comes from the opposite sex, one's peers or a larger community, rejection *hurts*. King is not superhuman, and it's worth remembering that negative reviews or harsh criticism are no less painful for him to hear than they would be to any novice author. But the difference, perhaps, is that King doesn't allow any of this to interfere with his writing. At all. In fact, he uses the negative and disparaging words of others as *fuel* to power his further ambition.

While it's perfectly OK to feel upset when you are turned down, criticized or found wanting, King shows us the only thing that really matters is that you persevere. There will always be someone who dislikes the work we do, but so what? By the same token, there will always be someone who appreciates and adores it—why not focus on those people?

Once again, we see that, contrary to what we might have internalized along the way, a big ego and success seldom go together. Humility and hard work have a greater success rate than grand plans that never materialize because the planner is unwilling to get messy, fail, or put the hours in. At the heart of it is fear. Fear in all its forms can hold us back, and make us doubt ourselves. We cannot live without fear, but we can learn the proper attitude toward it: that it never gets to decide what we do, and it certainly never gets to tell us what we're worth. Fear is normal and inevitable. But there's no reason to let it control or limit us.

If we can accept fear (maybe "get comfortable with it" is going too far!) we can turn our attention to other things that matter—like *why* we want to create in the first place, and what values we want our life to be guided by. Like Edison and Dyson, King simply came to accept that fear was part of the process. Self-doubt doesn't mean you have to abandon your dreams, it just means you are human. It may even be that King learnt all this in the first place by having someone else—his wife—believe in him when even he himself didn't.

Though nobody would argue that it's a good idea to put your self-worth in someone else's hands, there's a lot to be said for surrounding yourself with people who believe in you and will support you, or even push you when necessary. Critics can destroy a person's vision, but genuine and thoughtful supporters can build it up until you're strong enough to trust yourself.

If you find that ego and fear of rejection are holding you back in life, a counterintuitive way to tackle it is to avoid criticizing others. When we disparage another person's efforts or creations, we are really expressing our own attitudes toward thinking out of the box, making a mistake or trying something a bit brave. Do you mock or denigrate others? If so, you may find that being kinder and more compassionate paradoxically makes it easier for you to be kind to yourself. Your self-discipline efforts may come down to constantly reminding yourself that the only real critic is *you*—will you give yourself permission to try, to fail, to experiment? Or will you take a hostile attitude to things that are new and experimental?

Benjamin Franklin and ironclad schedules and goals

One final historical figure who provides a fantastic example of how to embrace self-discipline is none other than Benjamin Franklin. He's still the supreme example of an autodidact: a statesman, inventor, philosopher, writer, and polymath whose curiosity knew no limits.

Franklin was fastidious about keeping track of his goals, activities, and schedules, and he used them to navigate his personal and professional life. Two of his daily techniques for arranging his life are perfect for those looking to improve their organizational skills for better learning. Both were laid out in detail in Franklin's autobiography, perhaps with the hope of inspiring future generations to similar levels of achievement and productivity.

The first and probably more famous of Franklin's forms is his "thirteen virtues" checklist, which he used to chart his efforts in bettering himself as a human being. Although he used the thirteen virtues for self-improvement—or, as Franklin put it, "attaining moral perfection"—they serve as a strong example of how to mindfully track progress and keep records of anything you want to develop, including self-learning.

First, Franklin devised a list of thirteen qualities he felt he needed to develop in order to live a healthy and conscientious life when he was twenty years old (a freakishly young age to display such maturity, if you ask me). They included merits (not relevant to this chapter's discussion but helpful for illustration):

1. **Temperance**. Eat not to dullness; drink not to elevation.
2. **Silence**. Speak not but what may benefit others or yourself; avoid trifling conversation.
3. **Order**. Let all your things have their places; let each part of your business have its time.
4. **Resolution**. Resolve to perform what you ought; perform without fail what you resolve.
5. **Frugality**. Make no expense but to do good to others or yourself; i.e., waste nothing.
6. **Industry**. Lose no time; be always employ'd in something useful; cut off all unnecessary actions.
7. **Sincerity**. Use no hurtful deceit; think innocently and justly, and, if you speak, speak accordingly.

8. **Justice**. Wrong none by doing injuries, or omitting the benefits that are your duty.
9. **Moderation**. Avoid extremes; forbear resenting injuries so much as you think they deserve.
10. **Cleanliness**. Tolerate no uncleanliness in body, clothes, or habitation.
11. **Tranquillity**. Be not disturbed at trifles, or at accidents common or unavoidable.
12. **Chastity**. Rarely use venery but for health or offspring, never to dullness, weakness, or the injury of your own or another's peace or reputation.
13. **Humility**. Imitate Jesus and Socrates.

He then devised a system by which he strove to improve in each area in a very deliberate, methodical way. Coming up with the idea for the list itself is revolutionary in a way, since it focused his attention on what he was trying to accomplish. It was also a tall task—how many goals are you currently working on right now? Is it anywhere close to thirteen? It's time to rethink what is possible.

Franklin drew up a series of cards, each of which contained a very simple table with seven columns and thirteen rows. Heading each column were the seven days of the week: Sunday through Saturday. At the head of each row were symbols for each of his thirteen virtues. At the top of the entire page, Franklin wrote down the virtue that he chose to pay particular attention to for the duration of the week. The first week, he chose to focus primarily on temperance.

At the end of each day of the week, Franklin took out this card, reviewed the matrix, and put a black dot in each square for every instance during the day that he felt he "fell short" of maintaining that virtue. For example, if he felt he'd had a few too many glasses of wine at a Thursday dinner, he'd put a black dot in the "temperance" box for Thursday. If he decided he'd gotten a little too ticked off at George Washington at a Saturday meeting, he might put a black dot in the Saturday "tranquility" box.

In any given week, Franklin primarily focused on the virtue he entered at the top of each card. His reasoning was that cultivating one virtue at a time would make next week's virtue a little easier to handle, and that each virtue would become a habit in time. Each was carefully scheduled so that one week's virtue would help inform the next week's—for example, he put "frugality" the week before "industry" because he thought the habit of saving money would support his habit of working harder to obtain money. One at a time ensured that he wouldn't be overwhelmed and could discover what it took him to change a singular aspect of his life.

After Franklin had worked his way through thirteen weeks of checklists, he'd start over and begin a new series with his top virtue. He repeated all of his virtue exercises as he needed. If he faithfully did this every week, that meant he'd perform the task four times a year (13 weeks × 4 = 52 weeks = 1 year). Really, you just have to stand back and admire how neatly Franklin worked a calendar.

The genius of Franklin's checklist is that this approach works for other things besides becoming a better human being (though that's certainly a fine pursuit to try). Intentional planning, honest self-monitoring, and devotion of time without distraction is the name of the game.

For many of us still, this is a level of attention and self-awareness that is unheard of. We tend to think of our behavior as inborn and relatively unchangeable—but that's not the case if you don't want it to be the case, like Franklin. This type of intentional development and improvement underlay his success and accomplishments. You can also use it to track progress and chart your tasks in anything, including individual subjects of self-learning.

For example, if you're teaching yourself about the Spanish language and culture, you might come up with a few "planks" of your studies that you want to make sure you cover as much as possible: "reading," "writing," "audio practice," "social studies," "music/art," and so on. It might not make sense to cover each of these areas every single day, but at least a certain number of times each week would be helpful. Instead of focusing on a "Virtue of the Week" as Franklin did, maybe you'd pick a certain aspect of Spanish studies to focus on—"food," "history," "politics," "sport," "art," "manners"—whatever you know you'll be covering and could organize in a weekly cadence.

The key to this system's success is knowing what aspects of your studies are the most important to maintain—the same way Franklin decided what virtues were most essential for him to build on. Each subject will have different areas of importance. Separate them out and organize a plan of attack that ensures all your bases are covered. Your brain can only handle so many things at once, so plan yourself out of overwhelm and multitasking. Progress and learning in any regard require a steady march, even one that is tracked by weeks and years as Franklin's thirteen virtues were.

Don't just do what you *feel* like or whatever pops into your mind—be methodical and make sure nothing slips through the cracks. This is the purpose of the syllabus and schedule for a class in traditional education. Be sure to create your own to keep yourself on track and be an effective self-learner.

As Franklin himself noted, the real value of this system is to instill better habits on a rolling, gradual basis. Any kind of study system is extremely dependent on how well you nurture positive habits, and this is exceptionally true with self-learning since you're in charge of monitoring *everything*.

But we're not done with Benjamin Franklin yet, the famed proponent of the turkey as the national bird of the United States. How did he manage to accomplish so many great things in an almost countless number of areas?

The second part of his planning genius stems from the daily schedule he kept for himself. In his biography, Franklin also took the time to map out his schedule for each day, from waking up to bedtime. For example, one of his typical schedules (partially paraphrased) looked like this:

- *5:00 a.m. to 8:00 a.m.*: Rise, wash, "address powerful goodness" (pray or meditate), schedule the day, "prosecute the present study" (study and research whatever projects he was pursuing besides work), eat breakfast.

- *8:00 a.m. to 12:00 p.m.*: Work.

- *12:00 p.m. to 2:00 p.m.*: Read, "overlook my accounts" (attend to his personal or financial business), eat lunch.

- *2:00 p.m. to 5:00 p.m.*: Work.

- *5:00 p.m. to 10:00 p.m.*: Reflect, eat supper, consider "what good" he'd done during the day, enjoy "diversion" like hobbies, music, or conversation.

- *10:00 p.m. to 5:00 a.m.*: Sleep.

This may not look like an especially precise schedule in comparison to the schedules we may keep today, considering the infinite numbers of appointments and meetings we tend to fill our calendars with. But it's a great example to follow because it allows room for everything necessary to one's mental well-being: it treats personal and recreational activities with the exact same importance as business and work. Everything Franklin did was directed: it had its proper time and context, and all his activities were vital to his development the same way his virtues were. In an ideal world, a schedule focused on self-learning wouldn't look too different.

Franklin also differentiated between work he had to focus on exclusively (in those bigger morning and afternoon chunks) and work he could do while he was doing something else, like overlooking his accounts and conducting his personal studies. That undoubtedly gave him some flexibility and ease when he could take care of affairs that were important but could be done at a less active pace among other relaxing activities, like lunching. Actually scheduling time for personal reflection—something most of us probably don't think to do—shows that he realized it was both a vital activity to pursue *and* that it had its place during the day, no more or less important than anything else on his docket.

Even with his somewhat slower pace of life (compared to our own, that is), Franklin didn't always strictly keep to his schedule. That's fine. I'm sure in his day, like our own, things just *came up*. The benefit of having that daily plan was that it made him happier to at least *try* to live according to a schedule. If he didn't have even an *idea* of what he wanted to accomplish on a certain day, he'd be lost.

Having a schedule helped Franklin feel more organized and productive, even if he didn't follow it 100 percent every single day. Simply having something to refer to with premade decisions can lend guidance and structure to a day that wouldn't exist otherwise. You see, it's when we are faced with too many decisions that we run into problems. Once you remove the presence of decisions with a detailed schedule, you are far more likely to go along with what needs to happen.

So using Franklin's overall concept for your own schedule, here are some guidelines you should follow:

- Give yourself a couple of daily blocks to focus on your primary work. But provide yourself as much flexibility as you need within those blocks to mentally wander. Large blocks of time are more forgiving and allow you the space to go where the wind takes you.

- Schedule some time for recreation, leisure, personal reflection, or socializing with family and friends. Franklin knew these aspects were crucial enough to make room for them, especially personal reflection and understanding what went well and what needed to change during the day. The brain can't run on full speed all the time.

- Treat your personal goals with the same respect as your professional goals—in other words, schedule your self-learning with the same priority as your other responsibilities.

- Spend a relatively equal amount of time planning, ruminating, analyzing, and preparing as you do actually taking action. What went well and what didn't? Make sure you're doing the *right* thing instead of the *easy* thing and that you learn from your mistakes and inefficiencies.

- Wash. Definitely find time to wash.

These two habits of Benjamin Franklin—creating overarching goals and plans and adhering to a daily schedule—are techniques we can emulate. Self-discipline isn't something you can wing; planning is paramount to self-discipline because it is inherently tedious and boring, and sometimes you just can't give yourself the choice to not work toward your goals. Take a cue from this famous founding father and protect yourself from your worst impulses.

Lightning Source UK Ltd.
Milton Keynes UK
UKHW022235150221
378843UK00005B/922